Facebook
for Grown-Ups

Second Edition

Michael Miller

800 East 96th Street,

Indianapolis, Indiana 46240 USA

Contents at a Glance

Facebook® for Grown-Ups, Second Edition

ISBN-13: 978-0-7897-4902-4
ISBN-10: 0-7897-4902-5

Library of Congress Cataloging-in-Publication data is on file.

First Printing: December 2011

Trademarks

All terms mentioned in this book that are known to be trademarks or service marks have been appropriately capitalized. Que Publishing cannot attest to the accuracy of this information. Use of a term in this book should not be regarded as affecting the validity of any trademark or service mark.

Warning and Disclaimer

Every effort has been made to make this book as complete and as accurate as possible, but no warranty or fitness is implied. The information provided is on an "as is" basis. The author and the publisher shall have neither liability nor responsibility to any person or entity with respect to any loss or damages arising from the information contained in this book.

Bulk Sales

Que Publishing offers excellent discounts on this book when ordered in quantity for bulk purchases or special sales. For more information, please contact

> U.S. Corporate and Government Sales
> 1-800-382-3419
> corpsales@pearsontechgroup.com

For sales outside of the U.S., please contact

> International Sales
> international@pearsoned.com

Associate Publisher
Greg Wiegand

Acquisitions Editor
Michelle Newcomb

Development Editor
Charlotte Kughen,
The Wordsmithery
LLC

Technical Editor
Vince Averello

Managing Editor
Sandra Schroeder

Project Editor
Seth Kerney

Copy Editor
Jovana San
Nicolas-Shirley

Indexer
Cheryl Lenser

Proofreader
Apostrophe Editing
Services

**Publishing
Coordinator**
Cindy Teeters

Cover Designer
Anne Jones

Compositor
TnT Design, Inc.

Table of Contents

Part IV: Sharing Your Life on Facebook

Part VI: Doing More with Facebook

About the Author

Michael Miller has written more than 100 nonfiction how-to books in the past two decades, including Que's *Absolute Beginner's Guide to Computer Basics, Windows 7 Your Way*, and *The Ultimate Web Marketing Guide*. He is also the author of Que's *Facebook Essentials* video and Pearson Higher Education's *Introduction to Social Networking* textbook.

Mr. Miller has established a reputation for clearly explaining technical topics to nontechnical readers and for offering useful real-world advice about complicated topics. More information can be found at the author's website, located at www.molehillgroup.com.

Dedication

To Sherry, we're not getting older—we're just getting better.

Acknowledgments

Thanks to the usual suspects at Que Publishing, including but not limited to Greg Wiegand, Michelle Newcomb, Charlotte Kughen, Seth Kerney, Jovana San Nicolas-Shirley, and technical editor Vince Averello. And, of course, to all my Facebook friends—whether I actually know you or not.

We Want to Hear from You!

As the reader of this book, *you* are our most important critic and commentator. We value your opinion and want to know what we're doing right, what we could do better, what areas you'd like to see us publish in, and any other words of wisdom you're willing to pass our way.

As Editor-in-Chief for Que Publishing, I welcome your comments. You can email or write me directly to let me know what you did or didn't like about this book—as well as what we can do to make our books better.

Please note that I cannot help you with technical problems related to the topic of this book. We do have a User Services group, however, where I will forward specific technical questions related to the book.

When you write, please be sure to include this book's title and author as well as your name, email address, and phone number. I will carefully review your comments and share them with the author and editors who worked on the book.

Email: feedback@quepublishing.com

Mail: Greg Wiegand
            Editor-in-Chief
            Que Publishing
            800 East 96th Street
            Indianapolis, IN 46240 USA

Reader Services

Visit our website and register this book at www.quepublishing.com/register for convenient access to any updates, downloads, or errata that might be available for this book.

Introduction

A confession:

I'm not as young as I used to be.

Back in the day, I used to be known as a young Turk, a whiz kid, a young man with potential. But I'm no longer Turkish, don't have a lot of whiz left, and long ago gave up on realizing that potential thing. I got older.

Somewhere along the line I acquired a big house and a bigger mortgage, got married (to my high school sweetheart), and inherited kids (well, stepkids) and grandkids (also stepped). I look at what all the younger people in my household are doing and realize that I'm not doing anything remotely like that anymore. I'm an old guy kind of set in his ways—including the way I use technology.

Now, I write a lot of books about technology. To some degree, how a 50-year-old person uses Windows is pretty much the same as how a 20-year-old person does; Windows is Windows, after all. I get by.

But there's this new thing called social networking. It's technology related because you have to use your computer (or, in the case of the youngsters, your cell phone) to do it. And from what I've seen, how the young people use social networking is quite a bit different from how my wife and I do it. There's a definite generational difference here—which is where this book comes in.

Facebook for Grown-Ups focuses on the biggest and most happening social networking site, Facebook, and how people of our generation are using it. Trust me; we don't use Facebook the same way our kids do. It's a different experience for us, and one that has to be learned.

Did you know, for example, that you can use Facebook to keep in touch with all your family members—including distant relatives? Or that you can find long-lost friends on the Facebook site—including that cute guy you had a crush on back in high school? Or that you can share your family photos with these friends and relatives? And keep them updated on what you're up to these days?

That's right, grown-ups use Facebook to get connected with the people we know today, as well as those we knew in years gone by. We also use Facebook to keep tabs on our kids, to drop them a note from time to time, and to see what mischief they're getting themselves into. (And they are getting themselves into mischief; trust me.)

The key is figuring out how to find all the people you want to find and to share all the information you want to share—without sharing *too much* personal information about yourself. There's a bit of a trick to doing the social networking thing while still maintaining a semblance of privacy online.

I try to cover all that in this book. My focus is on using Facebook, yes, but as responsible adults—not as carefree kids. Because, let's face it, we haven't been carefree kids for quite some time now. Sad, I know, but true.

How This Book Is Organized

If I did my job right, *Facebook for Grown-Ups* should be a relatively quick but useful read. It contains a lot of information about Facebook's various and sundry features with an emphasis on how us grown-ups use those features.

To make things a little easier to grasp, this book is organized into six main parts, each focused on a particular major topic:

- **Part I, "Getting Started with Facebook,"** provides an introduction to this whole social networking thing and helps you sign up for Facebook and find your way around the site.

- **Part II, "Facebook for Friends and Family,"** is all about finding and communicating with friends and family members on Facebook. You learn how to get back in touch with old friends (including that cute high school crush) and how to make new ones online. You even learn how to use Facebook to keep tabs (or spy) on your kids—really.

- **Part III, "Keeping in Touch with Facebook,"** is about the many ways to communicate with your friends and family. You learn how to post public status updates, exchange private messages, and even chat in real time—which might be the only way to get face time with your kids. I even talk about Facebook's new video chat feature, which is pretty cool.

- **Part IV, "Sharing Your Life on Facebook,"** is about all the things you can share with your friends and family on Facebook. You learn how to share photos, home movies, even birthdays and other important events.

- **Part V, "Managing and Protecting Your Facebook Account,"** shows you how to configure your account settings—including all those privacy settings you can use to keep your personal information private. I also discuss some "safe Facebooking" practices and help keep you safe and private on the Facebook site.

- **Part VI, "Doing More with Facebook,"** covers some slightly more advanced things you might want to do, including personalizing your Profile page, "liking" the page of an entertainer or company, using Facebook for business networking and job hunting, using Facebook applications and games, buying and selling merchandise in the Facebook Marketplace, and accessing Facebook from your mobile phone. I even discuss some alternatives to Facebook, in the form of Google+, LinkedIn, MySpace, and Twitter, as well as how to connect Facebook to other sites and services you use on the web.

Although I recommend reading the book in consecutive order, you don't have to. Read it in chapter order if you want (I think it flows fairly well as written) or read just those chapters that interest you. It's okay either way.

Conventions Used in This Book

I hope that this book is easy enough to figure out on its own without requiring an instruction manual. As you read through the pages, however, it helps to know precisely how I've presented specific types of information.

As you read through this book, you'll note several special elements, presented in what we in the publishing business call "margin notes." There are different types of margin notes for different types of information, as you see here.

Beyond the main text, I end each chapter with a kind of sidebar observation. These sections aren't necessarily factual, as the rest of the text is supposed to be; they're more opinion, looking at Facebook from my personal viewpoint. Take 'em or leave 'em; that's up to you.

One more thing: Facebook is a website, and websites seem to change the way they look and act on a fairly frequent yet unpredictable basis. (In Facebook's case, they changed the entire news feed and user profiles after I'd submitted those chapters to my publisher, which required massive rewrites during the editing stage. Thanks a lot, Facebook.) That means that what I describe in these pages might look or act a little different by the time you get around to reading it. So if I talk about a particular button that is now a link located somewhere else on the page, try to be understanding. You still should be able to figure things out.

Note

This is a note that presents some interesting information, even if it isn't wholly relevant to the discussion in the main text.

Tip

This is a tip that might prove useful for whatever it is you're in the process of doing.

Caution

This is a warning that something you might accidentally do might have undesirable results—so take care!

Get Ready to Facebook

Now that you know how to use this book, it's time to get to the heart of the matter. But when you're ready to take a break from marveling at how old your friends look in their Facebook profiles, browse over to my personal website, located at www.molehillgroup.com. Here you can find more information on this book and other books I've written—including any necessary corrections and clarifications in the inevitable event that an error or two creeps into this text. (Hey, nobody's perfect!)

MySpace in April 2008. Facebook is currently the number-two site on the entire Internet, with more than 400 million users of all ages. That's a pretty big deal.

So if you want to social network today, Facebook is the place to do it. Facebook is a big honkin' web community, a site that offers a lot of different ways to publicly and privately communicate with lots and lots of people.

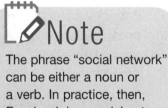

Note

The phrase "social network" can be either a noun or a verb. In practice, then, Facebook is a social network (noun) that lets you social network (verb) with your friends. Got it?

Chances are you already know a lot of folks who use Facebook. It goes without saying that your kids and their friends are all Facebook users; it's a rare youngster, indeed, who doesn't have Facebook as his browser home page. But it's not just the younger generation. You also find neighbors, coworkers, friends, and older family members using the site.

What Facebook offers is a collection of user profile pages, like the one in Figure 1.1. Every user has his own profile page, which functions as a sort of "timeline" to display this person's personal information, status updates, photos and videos, and even what pages they've visited and music they've listened to. When you become a "friend" of a person, you get access to their profile page and all that's on it. You have to ask people to be their friend; over time, you probably assemble a rather large list of such friends.

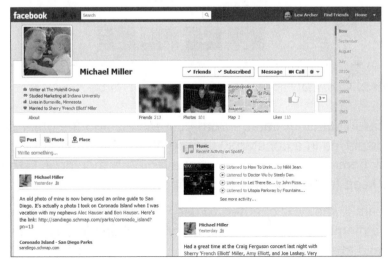

Figure 1.1. *A typical Facebook personal profile page.*

Facebook also offers profile pages for groups. A group can be a charitable organization, a company, or just an online club revolving around a specific topic. Facebook has groups for cat lovers, chess players, gardeners, and the like.

There are also Facebook pages for musicians, comedians, actors, television shows, movies, and the like; fans can follow their comings and goings via these pages. Similar pages exist for companies, brands, and products, where loyal customers can keep aware of what's happening market-wise. As with personal profile pages, these pages feature news about the topic at hand, photos, discussions, and such.

Figure 1.2. *An official Facebook page for musician Carole King.*

News—called status updates—from your friends and the other pages you like are displayed in a constantly flowing *News Feed* that appears on your Facebook home page. Everything that everybody's doing is listed there; it's how you keep track of all you deem important.

As you learn in the next chapter, to use Facebook you have to join the site— become a member, as it were. Facebook membership and use is totally free; all you have to spend is your time.

Things You Can—and Can't—Do on Facebook

Okay, so Facebook is the most popular social network. What does that mean to you—and what can you use it for?

Things to Do

First, you can use Facebook to let your friends and family know what you're up to. You do this in the form of short text messages called status updates. It's easy to log on and post a short status update; you can even do it from your cell phone!

Next, you can use Facebook to view all your friends' status updates. As previously noted, all these updates are consolidated into a single News Feed on your Facebook home page. Just open the www.facebook.com page, log in, and get updated on what all your friends are doing—via the News Feed (in the middle of the page) and a scrolling Ticker (at the top left) that tells you everything your friends are doing, in real time (see Figure 1.3).

Figure 1.3. *The News Feed and Ticker on Facebook's home page—lots and lots of status updates from all your friends.*

You can also use Facebook to communicate privately with individual friends. Facebook offers a built-in email system for private messages, as well as real-time instant messaging (Facebook calls it "chat") with online friends.

You can even conduct private video chats with your friends, which is way cool. So not everything you do has to be public.

That said, you can also use Facebook to share photos and videos. Just upload the files you want to share, and they're displayed on a link from your profile page, as shown in Figure 1.4. New photos and videos you upload are also displayed as status updates, so your friends receive notice of them in their News Feeds.

Figure 1.4. *A personal photo album, open for sharing on Facebook.*

Facebook also offers a way to announce and track important events, such as parties and gatherings, as well as invite your friends to these events. Of course, you can join any group you find interesting on the site, as well as play games, and do all sorts of other fun and marginally useful stuff. It's a fairly robust website, after all—a real community online.

Things *Not* to Do

With all the things you can do on Facebook, what sort of things *shouldn't* you do? That is, what sort of things is Facebook just not that suited for?

First, you have to remember that communicating with people via Facebook is no substitute for face-to-face communication. Those short, little status updates you make can't convey the same information as a longer letter or the emotion of a telephone conversation. Facebook communication is, at best, a kind of shorthand. When you really want to discuss something in depth, you need to do it in person, not on Facebook.

Then there's the whole issue of what constitutes a friend. A person you call a "friend" on Facebook might not be someone you'd even recognize if you ran into them in the grocery store. It's easy to deceive yourself into thinking you're immensely popular because you have a long friends list, but these folks aren't really friends; they're just people you broadcast to online. They're more like an audience than anything else.

This leads to the issue of whether online social networking is an effective replacement for real-world communication. You might be "talking" to more so-called friends online, but you might actually be talking to fewer real friends in the real world. Physical relationships could suffer if you spend too much time communicating virtually on Facebook; it's a false sort of familiarity that results.

And when you have hundreds of people on your Facebook friends list, how well do you really know any of them? It's possible, if not likely, that some of the people you call "friends" really aren't the people they present themselves to be. For whatever reason, some people adopt different personas—including fake names and profile pictures—when they're online; it's possible that you're establishing relationships on Facebook that have no basis in reality—which could result in online stalking or worse.

Bottom line, you shouldn't let Facebook replace your real-world friendships. It can supplement your friendships, make some general communication easier, and even help you renew old acquaintances, but it can never replace a good conversation with an old friend. That sort of connection is—and always will be—priceless.

Why Grown-Ups Use Facebook

Many people use social networks such as Facebook as a kind of container for all their online activities. I like to think of Facebook as an operating system. This is particularly the case with teenagers and college kids, who have Facebook open in their browsers all day long. They do almost everything from within Facebook—read status updates, send and receive emails, instant message with other users, share photos and videos, or play games. They never exit the site; it's as constant for them as is Windows.

Older users, however, tend not to be as Facebook-centric as the young'uns are. I don't know of too many people my age who are on Facebook 24/7, like their kids. We might check into Facebook a few times a day, but it doesn't monopolize our lives—or at least it shouldn't.

Instead, grown-ups use Facebook on a more occasional basis to keep tabs on what friends and family members are up to. We tend not to be as addicted to Facebook as our kids are; we don't have to know what everyone is doing on a minute-by-minute basis. Instead, we can log in once or maybe twice a day and get the general drift of everyone's activities. That's enough information for most of us.

Grown-ups also use Facebook to reconnect with people we haven't seen in a while—a long while, sometimes. Personally, I use Facebook to hook up with old friends from high school and college and to reconnect with former colleagues and those I might want to work with again. I guarantee you find people on Facebook that you haven't thought about for a long time (which might not always be a good thing, I suppose...).

Facebook is also a great place for family members—especially extended families—to keep abreast of comings and goings. It might take a lot of effort to write your cousins, and aunts and uncles, and nieces and nephews, and stepchildren, and in-laws, and all the rest, but a single Facebook status update does the job of multiple letters and emails. You can also use Facebook to share family photos with the rest of your family, which is tons easier than printing and mailing photos manually.

Speaking of family members, Facebook is a great way to spy on your kids. I don't mean that in a bad way, of course (or do I?); I mean that Facebook lets you see what your children are up to without them actually having to have a conversation with you about it. All you have to do is add your kids to your friends list, and you see all their status updates in your Facebook News Feed. (That is, unless they adjust their privacy settings to exclude you from their most private thoughts, which if they're smart, they'll do.)

Of course, there are plenty of ways for adult users to waste time on Facebook, just as our kids do. I know a fair number of supposed grown-ups who get addicted to *Farmville*, *Mafia Wars*, and other social games and spend way too much time playing them. So useless Facebook activity isn't the sole province of the young; us oldsters can also spend hours doing essentially nothing useful online.

Bottom line: Grown-ups use Facebook for many of the same reasons as younger folks do, but in a smarter and less intrusive fashion. Or so we'd like to think, anyway.

Other Social Media

Social networking is just one form of what the digerati call *social media*. (Who are these digerati, by the way?) Social media encompasses all websites, services, and platforms that people use to share experiences and opinions with each other.

In practice, that covers everything from social networks like Facebook to social bookmarking services, where users share the sites and articles they like. It also includes blogs, microblogs, and other forms of online communities.

Okay, that's a lot of jargon to just throw out there, so here's a bit of background.

A *social bookmarking service*, like Digg or Delicious, lets users share their favorite web pages with friends and colleagues online. When you join one of these social bookmarking services, you visit a website, web page, news article, or blog post that you like and then click a button or link to *bookmark* that site. This bookmark then appears in your master list of bookmarks on the social bookmarking service site; you can share any or all bookmarks with anyone you like.

A *blog* (short for "web log") is a shared online journal consisting of entries from the site's owner or creator. Bloggers create posts of varying length; some posts are just a sentence or two, others several paragraphs long; blog posts can include text, photos, and videos. Most blogs are focused on a specific topic, and some are almost journalistic in their execution. (Others read like personal diaries, so there's a bit of variety out there.)

A *microblogging service* essentially separates the status updates from everything else offered on a social network. Microblogs exist solely to distribute short text posts from individual users to groups of followers. These posts are similar to traditional blog posts but much shorter. The most popular microblogging service is Twitter, which lets you make posts (called *tweets*) of 140 characters or less—but that's all. No groups, no communities, no nothing else—just tweets.

Then we come to social networks, such as Facebook, which offer pretty much everything you find in other social media, but all in one site. Although you can keep a separate blog, create social bookmarks, and microblog to your heart's content on Twitter, if you want to do it all in one place, a general social networking site, like Facebook, is the better deal.

Chapter 2

Signing Up and Getting Started

Now that you've read the first chapter and learned what Facebook is all about, it's time to sign up to start using the site. What does that entail?

Before You Sign Up

Here are two nice things about using Facebook: It's easy, and it's free. That's right, even though you have to create an account, it's a free account; you never pay Facebook anything to use the site. That's because Facebook, like most websites these days, is totally advertiser supported. So you see some ads after you get on the site, but you aren't out a single penny.

What do you need to sign up? Not much, really. You need a working email address, a first and last name, and a birthdate. You also need to know your gender (I hope you already do) and come up with some sort of password you want to use. That's about it, really. Pretty simple.

Now, after you create your account, Facebook prompts you to enter all sorts of personal information. This includes everything from your street address and phone number to which books and movies you like. Fortunately, none of this info is mandatory; you don't have to enter any of this if you don't want to. (In fact, I recommend you *don't* enter a lot of the overly personal information; it's best not to publicize your contact information, for example.)

So you don't need to do a lot of prep work before you sign up. Assuming that you have a name and an email address, you're now ready to go.

Creating a Facebook Account

As I said, just about anyone can create a free Facebook account. All you have to do is follow these steps:

1. Go to the Facebook home page at www.facebook.com, as shown in Figure 2.1.

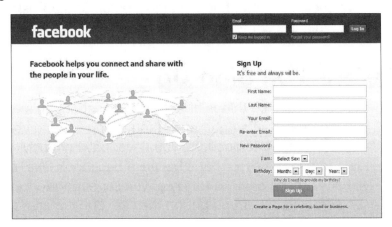

Figure 2.1. *Getting ready to create a new account from the Facebook home page.*

2. Enter your first name into the First Name box.

3. Enter your last name into the Last Name box.

4. Enter your email address into the Your Email box, and then enter it again into the Re-Enter Email box.

> **Note**
>
> You use your email address to sign into Facebook each time you enter the site.

5. Enter your desired password into the New Password box. Your password should be at least six characters long.

6. Select your gender from the I Am (Select Sex) list.

7. Select your date of birth from the Birthday (Month/Day/Year) list.

8. Click the Sign Up button.

9. When prompted to complete the Security Check page, enter the "secret words" from the *CAPTCHA* into the Text in the Box box, and then click the Sign Up button on this page.

10. Facebook now sends you an email message asking you to confirm your new Facebook account; when you receive this email, click the link to proceed.

That's it—you now have a Facebook account. But Facebook isn't done with you quite yet. Read on to learn more.

Find Friends and Complete Your Profile

When you confirm your new Facebook account, Facebook prompts you to find friends and family who are already on Facebook. You're also prompted to add more information to your Facebook profile.

Now, you don't have to do any of these things; you can skip any or all of these next steps, by clicking the Skip or Skip This Step link on any given page. But if you have a few free moments, you might as well get this stuff out of the way.

Here's how it works:

1. The first page you see is shown in Figure 2.2. This page is designed to help you find friends who are already on Facebook, by searching your web-based email contact list. Enter the email address for your email account into the Your Email box, and then click the Find Friends button.

Tip

To make your password more secure (harder for someone else to guess, that is), include a mix of alphabetic, numeric, and special characters (like punctuation marks). Longer passwords are also more secure.

Note

A CAPTCHA is a type of challenge-response test to ensure that you're actually a human being, rather than a computer program. You've seen lots of these things on the Web already; they typically consist of warped or otherwise distorted text that cannot be read by a machine or software program. Websites use CAPTCHAs to cut down on the amount of computer-generated spam they receive.

Note

Learn more about the friend-finding process in Chapter 4, "How to Find Old Friends—and Make New Ones."

Figure 2.2. *Searching for email contacts to add as friends.*

2. Facebook lists people in your email contacts list who are also members of Facebook. To add one or more of these people to your Facebook friends list, check the box next to that person's name, and then click the Add Friend or Add as Friends button. If you do not want to add any of these people, click Skip.

Note

This first step is for web-based email only, such as Hotmail, Gmail, or Yahoo! Mail.

3. Facebook displays a list of your email contacts who are not yet members of Facebook. To invite any of these people to join Facebook, check the box next to that person's name, and then click the Invite to Join button.

4. Facebook now displays the Step 2: Profile Information page, as shown in Figure 2.3. This is where you start filling in your personal information to be displayed in your Facebook profile. If you want to do this, start by typing the name of your high school into the High School box. A list of matching schools now appears; click to select yours from the list. When the Class Year list appears, select the year you graduated.

Tip

As you type into many boxes in the Facebook site, items that match what you're typing automatically appear in a list beneath the box. You can select the appropriate item from the list, if it's listed there, or just finish typing the complete name.

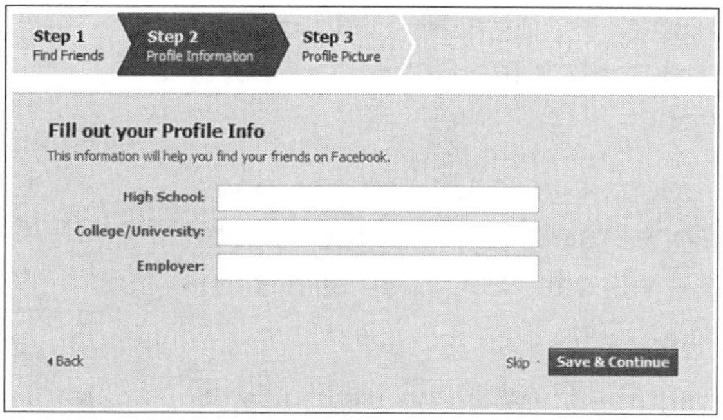

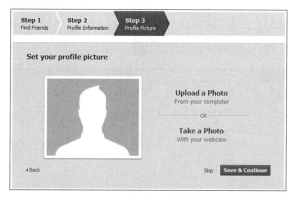

Figure 2.3. *Entering school and work information.*

5. If you graduated from or are attending a college or university, type the name of your college into the College/University box, and select the year of your graduation from the Class Year list.

6. If you are currently employed, type the name of your employer into the Employer box.

7. Click the Save & Continue button.

8. If you entered any school or work information, you are prompted to add people you might know from those schools or businesses as friends. (Facebook is a bear about adding friends.) If you so want, click the names of any people you know and want as friends, and then click the Save & Continue button.

9. Facebook now displays the Step 3: Profile Picture page, as shown in Figure 2.4, where you're prompted to set your Profile picture. Assuming you want to do this now and that you want to use an existing photo stored on your computer, click the Upload a Photo link.

Figure 2.4. *Getting ready to add your picture to your Facebook profile.*

10. When the Upload Your Profile Picture dialog box appears, click the Choose File or Browse button.

11. When the Choose File to Upload or Open dialog box appears, navigate to and select the photo you want to use. Then click the Open button.

12. When your picture appears on the page, click the Save & Continue button.

That's it, finally. You're now taken to a special Welcome page on the Facebook site, where you can start filling in your profile information.

Filling Out Your Profile

The next thing you want to do is fill out the personal information that appears in your Facebook profile. There's a lot about yourself you can enter, although most of it is optional—so you don't have to divulge too much, if you don't want.

You start this process on your own profile page. Here's how it works:

1. Click your name in the blue navigation toolbar at the top of any Facebook page.

2. This displays your profile page, as shown in Figure 2.5, which is fairly blank. Click the Update Info button.

Note

If your computer has a webcam built in or connected, you can use your webcam to shoot a new photo for your Facebook Profile. From the Step 3: Profile Picture page, click the Take a Photo link. When the Take a Profile Picture window appears, smile and click the Camera icon. After the countdown has been completed, click the Save Picture button.

Note

You can upload pictures in the JPG, GIF, or PNG formats, up to 4MB in size.

Figure 2.5. *Your empty profile page, ready for you to update your info.*

3. You now see your profile page in editing mode, as shown in Figure 2.6. Start with the Work and Education panel. Enter your current and any previous employers, where you went to college, and where you went to high school. Click Done Editing to proceed.

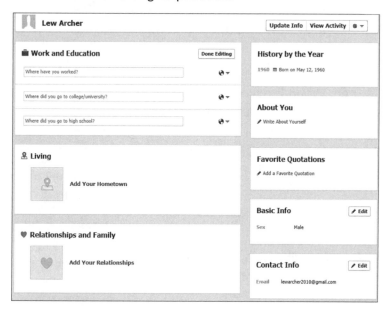

Figure 2.6. *Editing your profile page.*

4. Go to the Living panel and click Add Your Hometown. You can now enter your current city and hometown; click Save when done.

5. Go to the Relationships and Family panel, and click Add Your Relationships. Use the panel that now displays to select your relationship status (single, engaged, married, and so on) and to enter the names of your family members and their relation to you. Click Save when done.

6. Go to the About You pane and click Write About Yourself. When the About Me panel appears, write a short biography or description of yourself, and then click the Save button.

7. Go to the Favorite Quotations pane, and click Add a Favorite Quotation. When the next panel appears, enter one or more quotes you admire and then click Save.

8. Go to the Basic Information pane, and click the Edit button. When the next panel appears, confirm your gender and birthday, determine whether you

want to show your full birthday on the time-line on your profile page, check whether you're interested in men or women (or both, I presume), enter any languages other than English that you speak, enter your religious beliefs and political views, and then click Save.

9. Go to the Contact Info pane, and click the Edit button. When the next panel appears, enter any additional contact information (besides your main email address) that you want to share with your Facebook friends—IM screen names, phone numbers, street address, or website URL.

10. If you speak any languages other than English, enter them into the Languages box.

11. If you feel like it (it's optional), write a short note telling about yourself into the About Me box.

Remember, all this information is optional. You don't have to—and probably don't want to—enter any specific item. It's up to you how much of yourself you share with others on the Facebook site.

Selecting Privacy Level

Each item in your profile can be viewed by anybody on Facebook—or no one. It's all a matter of which privacy level you select.

I discuss privacy in more detail in Chapter 15. For now, know that there's a privacy button next to every item while you're editing your profile. Click this button to display the privacy options shown in Figure 2.7. You can select from the following:

Tip

If you want your friends to be reminded of your birthday, but not necessarily know how old you are, select Show Only Month & Day in My Profile.

Caution

Be cautious about providing any contact information to Facebook and other websites. You don't want to make it easy for unwanted people to contact you in the real world. Learn more about protecting your online privacy in Chapter 15, "Keeping Some Things Private: Managing Facebook's Privacy Settings."

Note

You don't have to enter all your profile information at this time. You can go back at any time and enter more information or change the information you've already added. Learn more in Chapter 14, "Managing Your Facebook Account."

Figure 2.7. *Determining who can view your profile information.*

- **Public.** Anyone on Facebook can see this information.

- **Friends.** Only your Facebook friends can see this information.

- **Only Me.** No one (except for you, of course) can see this information.

- **Custom.** Click this options to select specific individuals who can see this information—or specify people who will not be able to view this info.

In addition, Facebook displays any friends lists you've created or Facebook has created for you. (More on friends lists in Chapter 7, "Organizing Groups of Friends.") Select any given list to display this information to the people in that list.

The point is that you don't have to let everyone view everything about you. Be selective about what personal information you make public.

Creating Multiple Facebook Accounts

Here's something you probably didn't know you could do. For whatever reason you might have (and there are a few), you can actually create multiple Facebook accounts. All you need is multiple email addresses.

You see, Facebook bases each individual account on a unique email address. If you have more than one email address (and most of us do), you can create one Facebook account for each address. So, for example, if you have both work and home email addresses, you can create Facebook accounts for each.

(Technically, creating multiple accounts is a violation of Facebook's terms of service, but how are they supposed to know? I say go for it if you want; even if you get caught, you can always establish yet another account with another email address.)

Why might you want to create more than one Facebook account? It all has to do with having multiple identities online. For example, you might want to create both a personal and a professional persona on the Facebook site, so you can post your personal musings under one ID and your more professional thoughts under another. Or you might want to create a completely fictitious persona to track the online activities of your children. (More about that in Chapter 6, "Keeping Tabs on Your Kids.") Or if you're really creepy, you can just create multiple identities to play around with. Whatever floats your boat.

In any case, as long as you have distinct email addresses, there's no rule against creating multiple Facebook accounts. So have at it, if you want.

Chapter 3

Getting Around the Facebook Site

After you've signed up for Facebook, it's time to get to know the Facebook site. There's a lot there, if you know where to find it—which is what we discuss in this chapter.

What's What and What's Where on Facebook

When it comes to getting around the Facebook site, where should you start? Well, the logical place to start is the sign in page, and then what you see afterward—Facebook's home page.

Signing In

Point your web browser to www.facebook.com, and you see the Facebook sign in page, as shown in Figure 3.1. (This is also the page you used to register for Facebook, in case you forgot.) Signing in is as easy as entering your email address and password into the two boxes in the top right of the page, and then clicking the Log In button.

 Tip

If you don't want to be prompted to enter your login information every time you access the site, check the Keep Me Logged In option.

Check to stay logged in   Enter your password
Enter your email address   Click to log in

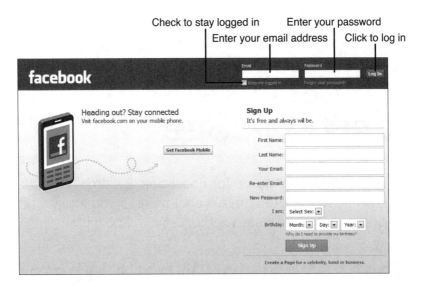

Figure 3.1. *Signing into Facebook—enter your email address and password.*

Welcome to the Home Page

After you've signed in, Facebook drops you right onto the Home page. This is as good a place as any to start your exploration of the Facebook site. It's also where you keep up to date on what your friends are doing.

As you can see in Figure 3.2, the Home page consists of three columns, a big one in the middle and two smaller ones on either side. We'll start on the left and work our way across the page.

The left column is one of your primary navigation aids to content on the Facebook site. Click a link here to navigate to a different section of the site.

What do you find in this navigation column? It differs a bit from user to user, but here are the most common elements:

- **Welcome.** This handy page for new users helps you enter profile information, find new friends, and the like.

Note

Facebook is constantly upgrading its feature set, so what you see might differ somewhat from what I describe here. And when Facebook adds to features, it sometimes rolls them out to selected users over time, so not every Facebook user sees the exact same pages. It makes life a little difficult for those of us who try to explain how Facebook works.

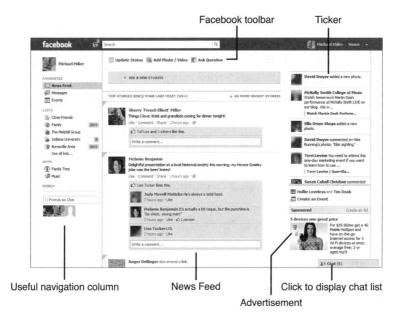

Figure 3.2. *The Facebook Home page—complete with News Feed of your friends' status updates.*

- **News Feed.** This is the default view on the Home page and where you view all your friends' status updates.

- **Messages.** All the messages you've received from other Facebook members, public or private, are displayed in this area. It's also the place you go to send new messages to other users.

- **Events.** This area displays any Facebook events you've signed up for and upcoming birthdays of your Facebook friends. You can also click here to create new events.

- **Lists.** This section displays links to various friends lists you've created or Facebook has created for you.

Note

Learn more about Facebook's messaging system in Chapter 9, "Exchanging Private Messages."

Note

Learn more about Facebook events in Chapter 13, "Sharing Birthdays and Events."

- **Apps.** Click the Apps link to display all the applications and games you and your friends are using. These are little widget-like utilities and games that add more fun and functionality to the Facebook site.

- **More.** Click this link to display links to Groups, Pages, Questions, Photos, Notes, Deals, and Links.

- **Friends on Chat.** This area is simply a list of all your Facebook friends who are currently online and available to chat. Click a friend's name to start an instant messaging-like chat with that person.

Lists are a good way to organize groups of friends. Learn more in Chapter about finding Facebook friends in Chapter 7, "Organizing Groups of Friends."

That's the left column. Now we get to the big column in the middle of the page, which contains the *News Feed*. The News Feed is, in essence, a scrolling list of status updates from your Facebook friends. At top of this list are

Learn more about Facebook games and applications in Chapter 20, "Finding Fun Games and Applications."

your Top Stories, those updates that Facebook feels you should be most interested in. These Top Stories are indicated by a blue triangle in the left corner. Other updates (what Facebook calls Recent Stories) are just below the Top Stories section, as shown in Figure 3.3; scroll down to view them.

Figure 3.3. *A Top Story (blue triangle) and Recent Story.*

By the way, if there are new non-Top Stories since your last visit, Facebook displays a More Recent Story link at the top of the Top Stories list, as shown in Figure 3.4. (That's so you'll know they're there, in case you don't scroll down automatically.) Click this link to view the new Recent Stories.

TOP STORIES SINCE YOUR LAST VISIT (3)	↓ 13 MORE RECENT STORIES

Figure 3.4. *Click the More Recent Stories link to view new non-Top Stories.*

And, just to confuse you even more, older Top Stories are displayed after newer Recent Stories. The News Feed, then, is in rough reverse chronological order, although Top Stories are given priority, wherever (or is it whenever?) they may appear. Just look for the little blue triangle to identify what might be the more important updates.

Note

Learn more about Top Stories, Recent Stories, and which is which in Chapter 5, "Visiting Friends and Family on Facebook."

The News Feed isn't the only place to find new information, however. At the top of the right column is something called the Ticker. This Ticker is a scrolling list of what your friends are doing, updated in real time. This list includes more than just status updates; it also includes comments your friends make on other updates, photos uploaded, songs listened to on Spotify and other music services, you name it. Just about anything Facebook knows about, however unimportant, is scrolled here.

Tip

Although you can scroll through the News Feed with either your mouse or keyboard, you cannot scroll through the Ticker with your mouse. To view older items, you need to first click on a visible item, then use the down arrow key on your computer keyboard to move down through the list.

Below the Ticker in the right column might be a variety of different items. For example, you might find a list of friends who have birthdays today; a list of upcoming events you're attending; a list of "people you may know" (and thus might want to add to your friends list); and some advertisements (in the "Sponsored" section). Aside from the Ticker, then, this column is a real hodge podge.

At the bottom of the right column is a little, blue box labeled Chat. Click this box to expand it into a full-fledged Chat pane that lists all your Facebook friends who are online and available to chat in real time.

Your Home page, however, might have a *fourth* column if your browser and monitor are wide enough. With a widescreen computer monitor and your browser extended to a fairly large width, Facebook expands the Chat list upward and into a new fourth column. Well, into the bottom half of this column, anyway. Facebook's Ticker moves into the top half of the new column. So you have Ticker and Chat in this new column, and everything else on the rest of the page.

And that, in a nutshell, is the Facebook Home page. It's more than just a gateway into the Facebook site; it's where you go to keep informed of your friends' activities. As such, it's the one page that most users always go to. I'd recommend bookmarking this page (which resides at www.facebook. com—after you've logged in, that is) in your web browser.

Profile Pages

Past the Home page, most other important pages on the Facebook site are individual users' Profile pages. A Profile page, like the one shown in Figure 3.5, contains a "timeline" of everything that user has done on Facebook, as well as displays that person's personal information, uploaded photos and videos, upcoming events, and the like.

Figure 3.5. *A typical Facebook Profile page.*

In essence, a Profile page is that person's home on the Facebook site. You have your own Profile page, of course, as does everyone else who's a Facebook member. You go to a friend's Profile page to learn more about that person or to view her information, photos, and such.

> **☐✎Note**
>
> Learn more about viewing a friend's Profile page in Chapter 5. Learn more about customizing your own Profile page in Chapter 17, "Personalizing Your Profile Page."

Navigating the Facebook Toolbar

As we just discussed, you can access many parts of the Facebook site from the navigation sidebar on the Facebook Home page. The other primary means of navigating the Facebook site is via the Facebook toolbar, as shown in Figure 3.6, that you find at the top of every Facebook page. It's a key way to get around the site.

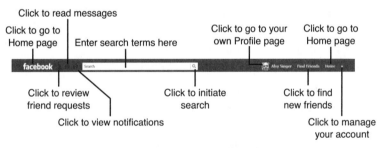

Figure 3.6. *The Facebook toolbar.*

What can you do from the Facebook toolbar? Here's a list, from left to right:

- Click the Facebook logo to go to the Facebook Home page, complete with News Feed.

- View any friend requests you've received. If you have any pending friend requests, you see a white number in a red box—for the number of requests— on top of the icon. Click the icon to view a drop-down list of these requests.

- View your most recent messages. As with the friend requests icon, a white number in a red box displays if you have unread messages. Click the icon to view a drop-down list of messages.

- View notifications from Facebook, such as someone commenting on your status or accepting your friend request. Click the icon to view the most recent notifications.

- Search the Facebook site for people and things. Just enter your query into the Search box, and then either click the Search (magnifying glass) button or press Enter on your computer keyboard (more on searching in just a sec).

- Visit your Profile page by clicking your name or picture.

- Click the Find Friends button (displayed on newer accounts only) to add new people to your Facebook Friends list.

- Another way to go to the Home page is by clicking the Home button on the right side of the toolbar. (Yes, this does exactly the same thing as clicking the Facebook logo; this button was requested by Facebook's Department of Redundancy Department.)

- Access all sorts of account settings, including important privacy settings, by clicking the Account button and then selecting an option from the drop-down menu. Options are Help Center (if you need help), Account Settings, Privacy Settings, and Log Out.

**Note**

Learn more about Facebook's privacy settings in Chapter 15, "Keeping Some Things Private: Managing Facebook's Privacy Settings." Learn more about Facebook's other account settings in Chapter 14, "Managing Your Facebook Account."

As I said, the Facebook toolbar appears at the top of every Facebook page. I use it primarily to jump back and forth between my Home and Profile pages. It's also useful to access your private messages and to search the site—and, of course, to access your privacy settings.

Searching Facebook

Let's talk a bit about searching Facebook. The Search box found in the Facebook toolbar can be used to search for virtually anything on the Facebook site.

That's right; Facebook uses a single Search box to search for all types of items. You can't fine-tune the search from the Search box; instead, you fine-tune the results when the results page appears.

How does it work then? Well, all you have to do is enter your query into the Search box. As you type, a list of items that match your query are displayed in a drop-down menu under the box, as shown in Figure 3.7.

Figure 3.7. *A list of suggestions appears as you enter a search query.*

If what you want is displayed in this list, great; click the item and go there. Otherwise, keep typing, and then press Enter or click the Search button.

Facebook now displays a search results page, like the one shown in Figure 3.8. By default, all items that match your query are displayed—people, groups, pages, events, you name it. You can, however, narrow down the results by type of item. Just click the type of item in the left column, and the search results of that type are displayed.

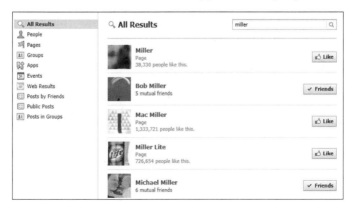

Figure 3.8. *A typical search results page.*

For example, if you want to display only people that match your query (that is, you're searching for a person), click People in the left column. If you want to display Facebook groups, click Groups. In this fashion, then, you can search for the following:

- **People.** You can choose to visit a person's Profile page (by clicking his name on the search results page), add that person as a friend (Add as Friend), or send that person a private message (Send a Message).

- **Pages.** These are what I like to call "fan pages," for companies and celebrities. You can visit a given page (by clicking the page's name in the search results) or choose to become a fan of that page (by clicking the Like link).

- **Groups.** You can visit a given group page (by clicking the group's name in the search results) or choose to become a member of that group (by clicking the Join Group or Request to Join links).

- **Apps.** You can visit that application's Facebook page, and from there, join the group by clicking the View App button.

- **Events.** You can visit an event's page (and then RSVP if you like) by clicking the event name in the search results.

- **Web Results.** That's right; these are web pages that match your query, as determined by Microsoft's Bing search engine. Click a link in the results to view that web page.

- **Posts by Friends.** This search displays your friends' status updates that match your query.

- **Public Posts.** To see all the status updates on Facebook that match your query—friends and otherwise—use this search.

- **Posts in Groups.** This displays status updates from people in your Facebook groups that match your query.

Of course, to display all these items at once, click All Results.

Signing Off

When you're done using Facebook and want to sign off from the site, all you have to do is click the Account button on the Facebook toolbar and then click Log Out. When you do this, you then have to log back in the next time you visit www.facebook.com.

You don't have to sign off, however. If you just navigate to a different website, and you checked the Keep Me Logged In option when you last signed on, the Facebook Home page is displayed when you next visit www.facebook.com. It's your choice.

Getting Help

There's one option on the Facebook toolbar I kind of glossed over. That's the Help Center option you see when you click the Account button. (You can also access the Help Center by scrolling to the bottom of any Facebook page and clicking the Help link.)

The Facebook Help Center is your gateway to information about every Facebook feature. There are guides to Using Facebook, Facebook Applications and Features, and Ads and Business solutions. Click the links in the Help Center sidebar to view guides to Games and Apps, Help Discussions, Getting Started, and Safety.

Even more useful, if you have a question about using Facebook, just enter it into the Search box on the Help Center page. This displays a list of FAQs (articles) and discussions that have something to do with what you're asking about.

And about these Help Discussions: These are questions asked by other users and answered by members of the Facebook community. I find these useful if "official" information about a given topic doesn't exist or is less than helpful. Just click the Help Discussion link in the Help Center sidebar, and then click a given topic listed.

As you'll see, there's a bevy of information available in the Help Center. Look here if you're having trouble finding something on the site or just don't know how to do something.

Chapter 4

How to Find Old Friends— and Make New Ones

Facebook is all about connecting with friends. In fact, the connections you make on Facebook are officially called "friends." You invite someone to be your friend; you add that person to your friends list; you manage your list of friends; and your News Feed displays the status updates of all your friends. Friends are part and parcel of the Facebook community.

Of course, before you can make someone your Facebook friend, you have to find that person on Facebook. That isn't always as easy as you might think, especially when you're looking for people you went to school with several decades ago. People move; women change their names when they get married (or divorced, or remarried, or some combination of the above); it's just darned difficult to track down some folks. This doesn't mean it can't be done, however. And if they're on Facebook, you can probably find them.

How Facebook Helps You Reconnect

When it comes to finding lost friends and family members, size is everything. That is, the more people there are in the community, the more likely it is that the person you're looking for is there.

And when it comes to size, Facebook is the biggest online community out there. 750 million users make for a pretty big pond; it's the one website that just about everybody signs onto, sooner or later.

The size of the Facebook community is both a good and a bad thing, of course. It's good in that it's so big that just about anyone you're looking for is probably a member. It's bad in that there are so many people to browse through that it's difficult to find any one individual. The person you're looking for is probably there, somewhere, if you only knew how to find him.

Fortunately, Facebook offers several tools for finding people on the site. First, Facebook can cross-tabulate your email and instant message contact lists with its own membership database, identifying your contacts who are also Facebook members. Second, you can search the site by name, although that can be somewhat frustrating when you're searching for someone with a fairly common name (try looking for "John Brown"—or "Michael Miller," for that matter). Finally, you can search for people by location (city or state), the school they went to, or the company they work or worked for; this is a good way to find former neighbors, classmates, or coworkers.

The end result is that you can create a Facebook network that consists of a fairly large number of people you used to know but haven't necessarily been in contact with for a while.

Personally, I've used Facebook to connect with many old high school and college friends; some of whom I hadn't talked to in more than twenty years. It took a bit of work, but after I made a few initial contacts, the others started to pour in. It's a matter of working through the connections, literally finding friends of friends.

That is, someone you know might be friends with someone else you know; this is particularly common when you're dealing with old school friends. After you connect with one friend, you can view their friends and find a lot of people you know in common. Knock down one domino, and they all start tumbling.

As a result, I now have more than 200 friends on Facebook, and I'm making more by the

Note

As far as Facebook is concerned, everyone you know is a "friend"—even family members. So when I talk about Facebook friends, these could be your siblings or children, people you work with, faint acquaintances, or even real friends. It's just a name.

day. Some of these friends are newer—people I know in the publishing and marketing communities—but many are my old schoolmates. I can't say they all look familiar, not after so many years (we all get older, don't we?), but I remember them all. Or most of them, anyway; the old memory isn't quite what it used to be.

Why Friends Are Important

Why are friends important? Well, I can't speak to the value of friends in real life (actually, I could, but this isn't the place for that), but I can tell you why friends are important on Facebook.

It's simple, really, and all about access. For a person to have full access to your Facebook Profile page and status updates, they must be added to your friends list. It's the same in reverse; you must be on that person's friends list to view her full Profile page and status updates.

In addition, when you add someone to your friends list, all of her status updates automatically appear on the News Feed on your Facebook Home page. Likewise, when you're added to someone else's friends list, all your status updates appear in that person's News Feed. It's a great way of keeping tabs on what your friends are doing.

Fortunately, there is no practical limit to the number of friends you can have on Facebook (okay, you can have up to 5,000 friends—a number you're never going to reach), so you don't have to pick and choose; you can make anybody a friend if you so want. Some people have hundreds of Facebook friends, whereas others have just a few. It's all up to you.

That said, there is no expectation that you dutifully read all the posts from all your Facebook friends. In fact, when you add a person to your Facebook friends list, that doesn't even imply that the person is a "friend" in the traditional use of the word. You might not even know that person; Facebook friends can be total strangers in real life. On Facebook, they're just people you follow—and who follow you.

Note

The process of finding new Facebook friends is called *friending*. When you remove someone from your friends list, you *unfriend* them.

Finding Friends with Connections

Let's start with the easiest way to find friends on Facebook—by letting Facebook do the work. Facebook knows who your current friends are, and who their friends are. Facebook also knows where you went to school, where you've worked, where you live, and a lot more about you, too. With this information in hand, Facebook can make the connections and look for other people who know your friends, other people who went to the same schools and worked at the same companies, and other people who live near you. All of these folks are potential friends.

To find friends with similar connections, follow these steps:

1. From the top of any Facebook page, click your name in the toolbar.

2. When your Profile page appears, click the Friends item near the top of the page, as shown in Figure 4.1.

Figure 4.1. *Getting to your friends from your Profile page.*

3. On the Friends page, shown in Figure 4.2, click the Find Friends button near the top of the page.

Figure 4.2. *Finding new friends.*

4. The next page displays a list of folks that Facebook thinks might be friends, as shown in Figure 4.3. These are typically friends of your current friends, and such. To invite any individual to be your friend, click the Add Friend button.

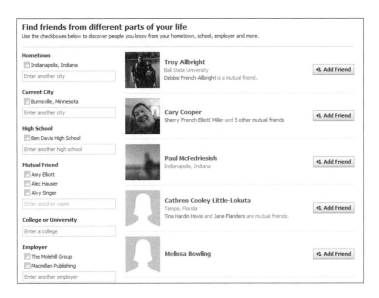

Figure 4.3. *Viewing potential friends—with connections.*

5.   You can search for friends based on a variety of criteria listed in the left column. Just check an item to display people who match that criteria. For example, to search for folks who you went to high school with, check the appropriate High School box.

Finding Friends via Email

If you recall, when you first signed up for your Facebook account, Facebook asked to look through your email contacts list for potential friends. You might have done this or you might not have; I typically ignore this step when I'm first getting started. In any case, there's a lot more looking that can be done, at any time you feel like it.

Even though today's high school and college generations seem to have abandoned email as being too slow and old fashioned (Email? Old fashioned already?), we oldsters still rely on email as a primary means of communicating online—especially for work and with family members. As such, it's a fair assumption that if you email someone on a regular basis, you might want to become Facebook friends with him.

To that end, Facebook can look through your email contact lists for people who are also Facebook members, and then invite those people to be your friends. Here's how it works:

1. If you have a Find Friends button in your Facebook toolbar, click it. Otherwise, click the Friend Requests button, and select the Find Friends link in the drop-down menu.

2. When the Friends Step 1 page appears, as shown in Figure 4.4, select the email service you use.

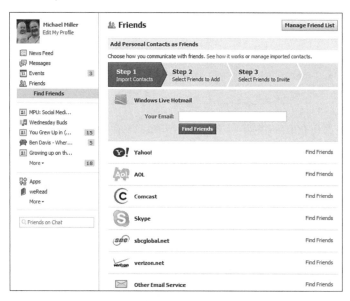

Figure 4.4. *Finding friends via email.*

3. If you use a web-based email service, such as Yahoo! Mail or Gmail, enter your email address and click the Find Friends button. (If prompted, enter your email password, too.) Facebook now displays a list of your email contacts who are also Facebook members.

Note

If you use Skype, you can also search your Skype contacts list for people on Facebook.

4. If you use Microsoft Outlook to check your email, click Other Tools, and then select Upload Contact File. When the page changes, click the Find My Windows Contacts button and follow the onscreen instructions to proceed.

5. If you use another software program to manage your email, follow the same instructions in Step 4, except click the Browse or Choose File button; then navigate to and select your email contacts file. When you return to the Friends page, click the Upload Contacts button to upload your email contacts list to Facebook and display a list of email contacts who are also Facebook members.

6. When the list of email contacts appears, as shown in Figure 4.5, check the box next to each person to whom you'd like to be friends.

Figure 4.5. *Identifying people you'd like to be friends with.*

7. Click the Send Invites button to send friend requests to these contacts.

Facebook now sends friend requests to the people you selected. When a person accepts your request, you become friends with that person. If a person does not accept your request, you don't become friends.

Searching for Long-Lost Friends

The preceding processes can find a lot of new friends for you. But what about folks who aren't already in your email contacts list, or who don't show up as a potential connection on Facebook.

Fortunately, Facebook lets you search for people by either name or email address. (Although, it's unlikely that you know the email address of someone you haven't seen in twenty years….) You can search for people from the search box on the Facebook toolbar or the one on the Friends page, although I prefer doing all my friend searching from the Friends page.

Follow these steps:

1. From any Facebook page, type a name or email address into the search box, and then click the Search button (the magnifying glass) or press Enter on your keyboard.

2. When the search results page appears, select People in the sidebar, as shown in Figure 4.6.

Figure 4.6. *The results of a friends search.*

3. To narrow your search to people who live in a given location, work at a specific company, or attended a given school, click the button at the top of the column and select either Location, Education, or Workplace. Then enter the given location, school, or company, and press Enter.

4. Click the Add Friend button next to the person to whom you want to send a friend request.

Tip

If the friend you're looking for has a relatively common name, such as John Smith, there might be too many people with that name on Facebook to find the correct one. It might be easier to search for that person by entering his email address, if you know it.

Accepting Friend Requests

Sometimes potential friends find you before you find them. When this happens, they send you a friend request, which you can then accept or decline. You might receive a friend request via email, or you can view friend requests within Facebook.

Here's how it all works:

1. To view pending friend requests, click the Friend Requests icon in the Facebook toolbar, as shown in Figure 4.7.

Figure 4.7. *Viewing pending friend requests.*

2. To view the Profile of a person requesting to be your friend, click his name.

3. To accept this friend request, click the Confirm button.

4. To refuse this request, click the Not Now button.

If you accept this person's request, he'll receive a notification as such. If you reject the request, the person will *not* be notified. This protects against negative reactions if you decide not to do the friend thing.

And here's the deal. You don't have to accept a friend request, even if you know that person in the real world. Remember, after you've accepted a friend request, that person can view all your personal information and status updates. (That is, unless you alter your privacy settings to hide information from that person, as I discuss in Chapter 15, "Keeping Some Things Private: Managing Facebook's Privacy Settings.") You might not want to accept all the friend requests you receive; that's your prerogative.

Finding Friends of Friends

Another way to find old friends is to look for people who are friends of your current friends. That is, when you make someone your friend on Facebook, you can browse through the list of people who are on his friends list. Chances are you find mutual friends on this list—people that both of you know, but you haven't found otherwise.

You find friends of your friends on your friends' Profile pages. Look for the box labeled Friends near the top of the page; these are the people on this person's friends list. Click the box to view all these people.

Click on any name in this list to view that person's profile page. To send a friend request to a person, click the Add Friend button. You'd be surprised how many old friends you can turn up this way!

Finding Hard-to-Find Friends

When it comes to tracking down old friends on Facebook, sometimes a little detective work is in order. It's especially tough to find women you used to know, as names get changed along with marital status. Some women have enough forethought to enter their maiden name as their middle name on Facebook—so the Cathy Coolidge you used to know might be listed as Cathy Coolidge Smith—which means their maiden names actually show up in a Facebook search. Others, however, don't do this—and thus become harder to find.

You can, of course, search for a partial name—searching just for "Cathy," for example. What happens next is a little interesting. Facebook returns a list of people named Cathy, of course, but puts at the top of this list people who have mutual friends in common with you. That's a nice touch, as it's likely that your old friend has already made a connection with another one of your Facebook friends.

Past that point, you can then display everyone on Facebook with that single name. But that's going to be a bit unwieldy, unless your friend has a unique name.

One approach to narrowing down the results is to specify a location in your search. For example, if you're looking for a John Smith and think he currently lives in Minnesota, you would search for "john smith minnesota." It's even better if you think you know a city; searching for "john smith minneapolis" narrows the results even further.

Other information added to your query can also help you better find people. For example, if you know where that person works, add the name of the company to the query. So if you think John Smith works at IBM, search for "john smith ibm."

Beyond these tips, finding long-lost friends on Facebook is a trial-and-error process. The best advice is to keep plugging—if they're on Facebook, you'll find them sooner or later.

Chapter 5

Visiting Friends and Family on Facebook

After you've found family members and old friends and made them part of your Facebook friends list, now what?

Actually, there's a lot that can happen next. First, you can keep up to date on your friends' daily comings and goings via the News Feed on your Facebook Home page. You can pore over your friends' personal information, photographs, and the like on their individual Profile pages. You can even leave comments on your friends' postings and leave your own messages.

It's all part of the community aspect of the Facebook community—and how you can get closer to your friends online.

Catching Up with the Facebook News Feed

Let's start by going home—to the Facebook Home page, that is. This is where you find a constant feed of status updates from everyone on your friends list. It's how you keep abreast of the latest developments regarding your friends.

Viewing the News Feed

When you sign into Facebook and open your Home page (www.facebook.com—or click the Home button on the Facebook toolbar), you see something called the News Feed. As you can see in Figure 5.1, this is a feed of the most recent status updates from people on your friends list.

Figure 5.1. *The News Feed on Facebook's Home page.*

Facebook divides the News Feed into Top Stories and Recent Stories. Top Stories are those updates that Facebook feels are most important; Recent Stories are everything else. You can tell a Top Story from a Recent Story in that it has a little blue triangle in the top left of the item.

What constitutes a Top Story? Beats me. Facebook has a super-secret algorithm that supposedly considers how often an update has been viewed, how many comments there are on it, how many friends the poster has, and who knows what else. Whatever the formula, I've found that Facebook doesn't always get it right; that is, the Top Stories I see in my News Feed often exclude posts from people I want to read about and includes posts that I'm totally indifferent to. Fortunately, you can fine-tune what appears in the Top Stories section of the News Feed; I'll tell you how in the "Fine-Tuning Your News Feed" section later in this chapter.

The status updates in the News Feed are displayed more or less in reverse chronological order. This means that the most recent updates are at the top and the older ones are at the bottom—with the notable exception that Top Stories appear before Recent Stories. To view even older updates, scroll to the bottom of the page, and click the Older Posts button.

What are you likely to find in a typical status update? Most updates are short text messages, although updates can also include photos, videos, notices of upcoming events, and links to other web pages. If there's a photo in a status update, like the one in Figure 5.2, click the photo to view it at a larger size. If there's a video in the status update, like the one in Figure 5.3, click the video to begin playback. If there's an event listed in the status update, like the one in Figure 5.4, click it to read more details and RSVP, if you're invited. If there's a link in the status update, like the one in Figure 5.5, click it to leave Facebook and visit the linked-to page. Pretty straightforward, really.

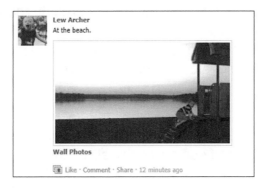

Figure 5.2. *A status update with a photo attached.*

Figure 5.3. *A status update with a video attached.*

Figure 5.4. *A status update with an event attached.*

Figure 5.5. *A status update with a link to another web page.*

By the way, if a friend posts from somewhere other than the Facebook page on his personal computer, you see this underneath the post, in the form of an icon for that particular device or service. Posts can also be made from cell phones via text messaging and via third-party applications, such as TweetDeck and Foursquare, that automate posting to Facebook and other social networking sites.

Your friends are likely to post about what they're doing and what they're thinking. Some people post once a day, some post once a week, some post several times a day, and some don't post much at all. There are no rules or guidelines as to how often people should post or what they should post about. To me, the best posts keep me updated on my friends' lives—what activities they're participating in, what their kids are up to, when they're sick or well, that sort of thing. But you never know what your friends will post, which is what makes it interesting.

Fine-Tuning Your Top Stories

Back to those Top Stories I discussed earlier. Facebook tries to figure out which updates you're most interested in but doesn't always get it right. Fortunately, you can help Facebook fine-tune those updates you see first in your News Feed.

When you find an update in your Top Stories list that you're *not* that interested in, hover over the story until you see a little down arrow on the right. Click this down arrow to display a menu of options, as shown in Figure 5.6. Click the Unmark as Top Story option, and this update is moved into the Recent Stories section—and Facebook learns from this action.

Figure 5.6. *Choosing further actions for a given story.*

If you see an update in your Recent Stories section that should be a Top Story, click that same down arrow and Mark as Top Story. This moves the story up top and helps Facebook select similar updates in the future.

Hiding Friends and Posts You Don't Like

You'll find that some of your Facebook friends post a lot. No, I mean it, *really* a lot. Not just once or twice a day, but seemingly hourly—and they seldom say anything remotely interesting.

This frequent, mindless posting is seldom a good thing. Some of my more annoying "friends" post about when they got up in the morning, what they had for breakfast, when they're fixing coffee, why they're feeling out of sorts, and when they're going to bed—way too much information, if you ask me.

Then there are those friends (that really aren't friends) who don't share personal information per se, but rather are using Facebook to promote themselves or their businesses. Fine and dandy, but at some point I just don't care.

Of course, there are also those businesses and celebrities that you've said you "like" on Facebook. Posts from these entities also show up in your News Feed, and some of these can be really annoying.

The point is, you might not always want to view status updates from everyone or everything that shows up in your News Feed. Fortunately, there's a way to filter whose updates appear in the News Feed by hiding updates from selected friends.

Hiding updates from a given person or entity is fairly easy. All you have to do is hover over an update from that person to display the down arrow to the right of the update. Click the down arrow and select Unsubscribe from *Friend.* Voilà—no more status updates from this person will appear in your News Feed, ever. Nice!

You can also hide individual status updates in your News Feed. Just click the aforementioned down arrow and select Hide Story. Simple as that—the item is no longer visible.

Displaying More—or Fewer—Updates from a Friend

When you "friend" someone on Facebook, you essentially subscribe to their posts. There are three levels of subscription—you can view All Updates, Most Updates, or Only Important updates. The differences between these three levels are subtle, but the default Most Updates works well for most people.

If you prefer to view more updates from a given person—pretty much everything they post—then click the down arrow next to one of this person's posts and select All Updates from the pop-up menu. If you don't want to see quite as much from this individual, click that same down arrow and select Important Updates, instead.

Hiding Updates from Applications and Games

Some status updates aren't really updates from that person, but rather updates from an application or game that the person is using or playing. For example, you might see status updates alerting you that a friend has achieved a certain level on *Farmville*, or killed someone in *Mafia Wars*, or read a new book in their Goodreads library.

I find these automatically generated updates extremely intrusive—especially from people who incessantly play these social games. It's possible to see update after update after update from a person playing a game, which just takes up valuable space in your News Feed.

Note

Learn more about Facebook applications and games in Chapter 20, "Finding Fun Games and Applications."

Now, you could decide to hide all posts from your game-addicted friend, but that would be throwing the proverbial baby out with the bath water; you'd also hide any important posts he might make. A better option is to hide posts from that game or application, so that you're never bothered by *Farmville* or *Mafia Wars* again.

Hiding posts from an application or game is similar to hiding posts from a person. Start by finding one of these annoying application-generated posts: then point to the post to display the down arrow. When the pop-up menu appears, click Hide All by *Application*. This hides all future posts from this application regarding *all* your friends. You can banish *Farmville* forever!

Commenting on Friends' Posts

Sometimes you read a friend's post, and you want to say something about it. To this end, Facebook enables you to comment on just about any post your friends make. These comments then appear under the post in your News Feed, as shown in Figure 5.7.

Figure 5.7. *Comments under a friend's status update.*

To comment on a friend's status update, simply click the Comment link under that post. A text box now displays, like the one shown in Figure 5.8. Enter your comment, and then press Enter; your comment now appears underneath the original post, along with comments from any other people.

Figure 5.8. *Adding a comment under a friend's status update.*

Liking What You See

Sometimes you want to voice your approval for a post but don't necessarily want to take the time to type out a comment. In this instance, you can simply click the Like link under a status update. This puts a little "thumbs up" icon under the post, along with a message that you "like this."

By the way, if you later decide you *don't* like that post, you can go back and remove your approval. Just click the Unlike link, and you won't be listed as liking it any more.

 **Note**

You can both like and comment on a post; they're not mutually exclusive.

Sharing a Posted Attachment

When a friend posts an attachment to a status update—a photo, video, event, or web page link—you can share that attachment with your friends on Facebook. You can share the attachment as a public post of your own or via a private message.

To share an attachment as a status update, follow these steps:

1. Click the Share link under your friend's status update. (This link appears only when an attachment is present; it isn't there for a standard text-only post.)

2. When the Share This *Attachment* dialog box appears, as shown in Figure 5.9, enter the text of your accompanying status update into the Write Something box.

Figure 5.9. *Sharing a friend's attachment as a new status update.*

3. Click the Share *Attachment* button, and you create a new status update with your friend's original post and attachment attached.

To share an attachment privately with another friend, follow these steps:

1. Click the Share link under your friend's status update.

2. When the Share This *Attachment* dialog box appears, click the On Your Own Wall button, and then select In a Private Message.

3. When the dialog box changes, enter the name of the recipient into the Enter a Friend's Name box. If you're sending to multiple friends, use commas to separate their names.

4. Enter an accompanying message into the Write Something box.

5. Click the Share *Attachment* button.

Your friend(s) now receive a Facebook message with the original status update and its attachment attached.

Subscribing to People Who Aren't Your Friends

This chapter is all about keeping up with what your friends are doing and saying. But you don't have to add someone to your friends list to follow their activities on Facebook. Instead, you can simply opt to subscribe to that person's public updates, and that person will never know you're following them. (Nice for stalking—or for surreptitiously keeping track of your kids' activities.)

When you subscribe to a person, you see all the updates that they choose to post publicly. You don't see those updates that go only to their friends lists. In fact, they never know you've subscribed to them.

In addition, the people you subscribe to don't see anything you post. (Unless they subscribe to you, of course.) It's a one-way sort of thing.

How do you subscribe to someone? It's as simple as navigating to that person's profile page and then clicking the Subscribe button. Now, this button is only visible if this person has allowed subscribers; not all people do. But if the option is available, all you have to do is click the button.

Note

The one-way nature of Facebook subscriptions is similar to the way you follow people on Twitter.

You can then select what kinds of items you want to see from this person. Hover over the Subscribed button to view and select from the following list:

- Life Events
- Status Updates
- Photos
- Games
- Comments and Likes
- Other Activity
- Music and Videos

In addition, you can choose the level of updates you see—All Updates, Most Updates, or Only Important updates. In this way you can fine-tune just how closely you follow this person.

Getting to and Getting to Know Your Friends' Profile Pages

Reading status updates in your News Feed keeps you up to date on your friends' latest activities. But what about older activities? Or if you want to look at any photos or videos they've uploaded? Of if you just want to view her personal information?

Everything you'd want to know about a Facebook friend is located on her individual Profile page.

Displaying a Profile Page

How do you display a friend's Profile page? It's easy: All you have to do is click that person's name anywhere on the Facebook site.

Where can you find a person's name to click? There are lots of places, including the following:

- In a status update in the News Feed on your Home page
- In the From: field of a message sent to you

- In a chat window when you're using Facebook's chat (instant messaging) feature

- In the Friends section of your own Profile page

- In the Friends section of another friend's Profile page

You can also find your friends in your all-inclusive friends list. To display a list of all your friends, like the one shown in Figure 5.10, go to your own Profile page, and click the Friends box. I'm not quite sure how this list is ordered, but it always seems to put first those friends with whom you either interact with most or have recently interacted with. In any case, you can use the search box at the top of the page to seek out specific friends. To display a friend's Profile page, all you have to do is click that friend's name in the list.

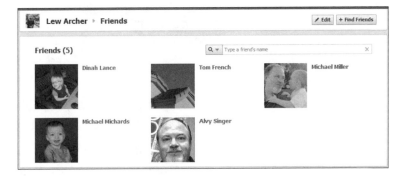

Figure 5.10. *Your friends list.*

Navigating a Profile Page

What do you see when you display a friend's Profile page? As you can see in Figure 5.11, a Profile page is actually a timeline to all of that friend's Facebook activities—in addition to displaying key information about that person.

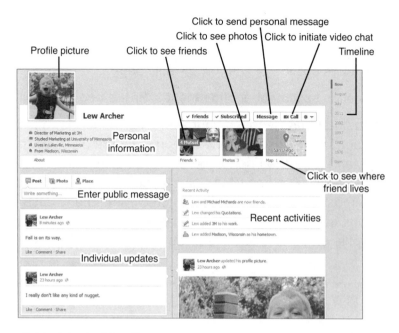

Figure 5.11. *A typical Profile page.*

There's a lot of interesting stuff here. Starting at the very top of the page, you can see your friend's profile picture along with a group of buttons:

- The checked Friends button means that, no surprise, you're friends with this person. Hover over this button to add this person to a specific friends list or unfriend this person.

- The checked Subscribe button means that you're subscribed to follow this friend's posts. Hover over this button to change the type of posts you see or to unsubscribe.

- Click the Message button to send this person a private message.

- Click the Call button to start a video chat with this person, if he's online.

- Click the Gear button for various friend-related activities, including blocking posts from this person.

Beneath the profile picture is a summary of key information about this person—where he works, went to school, lives, and so forth. Click the About link to view a full page of personal information, like the one shown in Figure 5.12, that includes full employment and education histories, favorite quotations, and such.

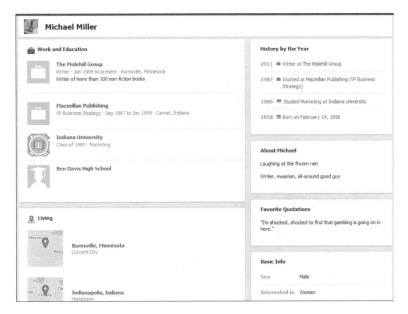

Figure 5.12. *Viewing a friend's detailed personal information.*

Back on the main Profile page, to the right of the summary information (just below the row of buttons) you see several large image boxes. Depending on the width of your web browser, you might see three or four or more boxes; click the down-arrow to see any boxes not currently displayed. These boxes include

- **Friends.** Click this box to view your friend's complete friends list.

- **Photos.** Click to view those photos your friend has uploaded. These photos are stored in separate photo albums, as you can see in Figure 5.13; click an album to view the photos within. (Beneath this person's photo albums is a list of photos in which this person has been tagged.)

- **Map.** Click to view a map of where your friend lives.

- **Likes.** Click to view your friend's favorite music, books, movies, and the like, as shown in Figure 5.14.

- **Notes.** Click to view any extended notes your friend has written.

- **Music.** If your friend has linked an online music service to his Facebook account, click this one to see what he's been listening to.

Figure 5.13. *Viewing your friend's photos.*

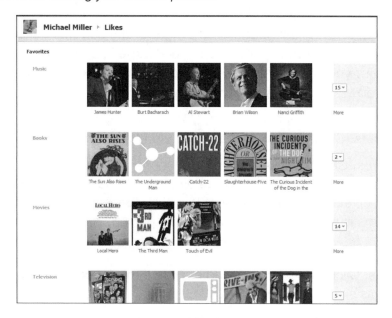

Figure 5.14. *Viewing what your friend's favorite things.*

In addition, any apps your friend has recently used may be listed here; click to view recent activity.

Beneath this top box of information are two long columns of activities—the most recent activities and such. At the top of the left column is a Write Something box; use this to post a message on your friend's Profile page. At the top of the right column is a Most Recent Activity box, which tells you what your friend has been doing recently. Regular items follow.

Depending on what apps your friend has linked to Facebook, you may also see boxes for those apps. For example, Figure 5.15 shows a Music box, linked from the Spotify service, that displays the most recent songs your friend has listened to. Kind of interesting, if not a little intrusive.

Figure 5.15. *Viewing a friend's recent music choices.*

You can view older items by scrolling down the page, or by using the timeline on the far right. This timeline runs from Now (at the top) to the earliest activity for this person listed on Facebook. (That doesn't necessarily mean his first Facebook post; the timeline goes all the way to the person's birthdate, if not earlier.) Click a year or month on the timeline to view all your friend's activity at that point in time. (For example, Figure 5.16 shows my own activity more than two years ago.)

Figure 5.16. *Viewing older activity on the timeline.*

Facebook intends for this Profile page to tell a person's "life story"—or as much of it as Facebook knows about, anyway. It's certainly an interesting way to keep up with what a friend has been doing over the years, all on a single web page. You can learn a lot from reading a person's full Profile page.

All Comments Are Public

I say this several times throughout the book, but it's important to remember that Facebook is a *public* website. That means that just about everything you do on Facebook is visible to everybody else.

This is especially true in the comments you leave on your friends' status updates. It's easy to trick yourself into thinking that leaving a comment is a bit like replying to a private email, but a Facebook comment isn't private at all. Any comment you make is visible to all your friend's friends and possibly to everybody else on the Facebook site. (This last possibility depends on how your friend has configured his privacy settings.)

If you think you're leaving a private reply, you're more apt to write something that you really shouldn't. Here's an example: I was reading the comments on a friend's page a while back and saw a comment to one of the updates there. A friend of my friend made a comment; my friend commented back, something along the lines of "how have things been going?," and the resulting comment was a long litany of how this person's wife was having an affair, how awful his life was, and on and on in that fashion. Obviously, this comment was not private because I was reading it, but the poster—the friend of my friend—either didn't know or care that his comment was a very public one.

The take-away here is that you shouldn't make any comment to any post that you don't want all your other friends to read. Facebook comments are not the place to post private messages; they're the Facebook equivalent of public announcements and should be treated as such.

Chapter 6

Keeping Tabs on Your Kids

Facebook is a great place to reconnect with old friends. It's also a great place to connect with family members—especially your children.

Now, this assumes that your kids are on Facebook, which they probably are. It also assumes that your kids want to be your Facebook friends—although there are things you can do if you're left unfriended.

The point is to not so much use Facebook as a way to communicate with your kids (although you can do that), but rather use Facebook to keep a watchful eye on what your kids are doing. Most young people use Facebook as a bit of a personal diary, posting all sorts of juicy details as to their private thoughts and activities; you can find out a lot about what your kids are up to just by reading their Facebook status updates.

Making Your Children Your Friends

The first step in using Facebook to watch your children is to add your kids to your friends list. This should be a fairly straightforward process—in fact, Facebook might suggest your children as friends when you first sign up, especially if you have your kids' addresses in your email contacts list.

Otherwise, you need to do a simple search for your kids on the Facebook site, as we discussed in Chapter 4, "How to Find Old Friends—and Make New Ones." You can search either by name or by email address, if in fact your kids have an email address and you know what it is. In any case, it shouldn't be too hard to find your children on Facebook, and then send out the necessary friend requests.

What to Do If Your Kids Hide from You on Facebook

What do you do if one of your kids refuses your friend request? Or what if your child takes you on as a friend, but uses Facebook's various privacy settings to keep you from seeing all the interesting stuff he posts online? (It can be done; it's easy enough to block certain "friends" from seeing some or all status updates.)

If you find yourself all or partly blocked from reading your child's Facebook status updates, pat yourself on the back; you have a smart, technically savvy, and understandably wary offspring. He knows that you're probably going on Facebook to keep an eye on his activities, and he thinks he can block you out by not making you his friend.

Fair enough, as far as it goes. But you still have a few options.

Viewing Updates Without Being a Friend

First, you might not even have to make your child a Facebook friend to view his Profile page and status updates. Many people configure Facebook's privacy settings so that all users can view their status updates. If your child is this negligent, you don't have to be a friend to read everything he posts. Just find and go to his Profile page and read to your heart's content. It's worth a shot.

Subscribing to Your Child's Updates

Facebook's subscription feature is relatively new, and not every user has activated it. But if your child has activated subscriptions, you can follow what he is doing without his knowledge.

All you have to do is subscribe to your child on Facebook. Go to his Profile page, and click the Subscription button (if it's there). Then you see all your child's public posts in your News Feed.

Know, however, that your child can still block you from some or all posts—if he thinks about it. Don't blow a good thing by mentioning that you've subscribed to his posts, or that you've actually read some of them. Loose lips sink ships and all that, so remain a viewer, not a participant.

Creating a Surreptitious Identity

Some youngsters are savvy enough (and care enough about their privacy) to configure Facebook's privacy settings to display their status updates only to friends. Some are even savvier and know how to block specific people— like you—from viewing their updates. What to do, then, if you find yourself locked out from your child's innermost Facebook postings?

Your only recourse at this point is to reinvent yourself—as someone else. That is, you need to create a second Facebook account under a different name and identity. Instead of being a forty-something mother, you need to be a teenage girl or a college-age dude. In other words, you need to become someone that your child won't automatically think to block on Facebook.

But wait—why would your child accept a friend request from a complete stranger, albeit one closer to his own age? Because, unfortunately, most teenagers and young adults have hundreds of Facebook friends, many of which they've never met in real life. They're friends of friends, acquaintances, people they bumped into once in the hall between classes, or folks who just happen to live nearby or go to the same school or work at the same company. For better or worse, younger users are accustomed to accepting friend requests without question, as long as there are no obvious "red flags" concerning the person making the request. So as long as you don't stand out as an old weirdo, chances are you can fake your way onto your child's friends list.

Establishing a new identity does require some creativity, of course. First, you need to get the age right; within a year either side of your child's age is generally good.

Next, the gender. Is your son more likely to accept a request from a pretty girl or a guy he's never met? (I'd bet on the girl.) Is your daughter more likely to accept a request from a cool girl or a good looking guy? (Not to be sexist, but this one is a tougher question; many girls are less questioning about Facebook girlfriends than they are guys they've never met.)

You need to pick a new name, of course, something age appropriate. (That means something hip like "Colby" or "Dylan" instead of the old-fashioned "Margaret" or "Robert.") Make sure the person you're inventing lives nearby; kids are less likely to make friends with people who live across the country.

As to school, this is also a little tricky. If your child goes to a smaller school where everyone is likely to know everyone else, you probably don't want to say you go to that school, too; instead, pick a neighboring school where he doesn't know everyone. If your child goes to a larger school, however, particularly a large university, you can fake the school allegiance and no one is the wiser.

Then you need to fill in some personal information. The new person you're becoming should have a lot of the same likes and dislikes as your child—television shows, movies, music, and such. If you don't know what your kid likes...well, shame on you.

Finally, you need to have a second email address, one your child doesn't know about. It shouldn't be easily traceable to you—that is, it shouldn't include your real name in the email address. I recommend creating a new account at one of the big web email services, such as Gmail or Hotmail, just for this purpose.

After you've created this new account for your fictitious self, you should first seek out some of your offspring's friends and invite them onto your friends list. Don't start by making your child your first and only friend; you need to establish your identity before you ingratiate yourself with your child. It helps if you have a handful of friends already established; then it looks kind of normal when you ask your child to join your friends list.

After you're on the list, you don't have to—and probably shouldn't—interact with your child.

Tip

You don't have to—and probably shouldn't—add a photo to your fake Facebook account. Not every Facebooker has a Profile picture, so the absence of such shouldn't be suspicious. On the other hand, choosing the wrong photo could set off warning alarms. Plus, where are you going to get the picture, anyway? You could get into more trouble ripping off someone else's photo than you could being found out by your child.

Most Facebook friends are silent friends, so it won't look odd if you don't comment on your child's updates or make updates of your own. Just keep to the background and observe as best you can.

Yes, it's spying, but you're a parent—you're entitled.

Using Facebook to See What Your Kids Are Up To

The whole point of using Facebook to keep tabs on your kids is to look and listen without doing a lot of talking. You kind of want your child to forget that you're there, so she lets her guard down. If your child thinks that you're watching, she'll be careful about what she posts. If she forgets a parent is watching, she'll be a lot more free with what she says on the site.

The main thing you want to do is read your child's status updates and view their photos. Most young people on Facebook, for whatever reason, are surprisingly open about what they post; you get to see who your child is hanging out with, hear about her latest fight with her boyfriend, read about how much she hates her classes this semester or likes her new job or is creeped out by the guy who works at the Sbarro stand at the mall. Your child's innermost thoughts, both profound and mundane, are there on her Wall for you to read.

It's kind of like eavesdropping on a private conversation—except that it's a public conversation that anyone can listen to. After all, your child's status updates are there on Facebook for everyone to read. You just happen to be actively interested in reading everything your child posts.

To be a successful parental Facebook stalker, however, you need to keep your presence muted. That is, you don't want to remind your child that you're reading what she writes. That means *not* commenting on your child's posts. This might be the hardest part of the whole process; most parents have to really restrain

Note

Just because you shouldn't comment on your child's status updates doesn't mean that you can't make new status updates on your own Profile page. Chances are your child won't equate your occasional post showing up in her News Feed with the fact that you're eyeballing everything she posts online.

themselves from offering advice or support or consoling their kids when they make a post. You can't do that. You just can't. You have to stay invisible on your child's Profile page, so she doesn't know that you're there.

If you can't resist the urge and do post a comment to one of your child's status updates, let me tell you what is likely to happen. First, your child will become much less open on Facebook; the number of posts she makes will drop dramatically. Then she'll get smart and figure out how to configure Facebook so that you—and you alone—can't read her status updates. Then she'll go back to posting frequently, but you'll never know because you won't be able to see a thing she posts. In other words, you'll have blown your cover.

So heed my advice and, after you get inside, stay silent. Yes, you'll be listed as one of her Facebook friends, but you'll be one of those silent friends she soon forgets about. Out of sight and out of mind, if you want to stay in the loop.

Using Facebook to Contact Your Grown Kids

All this talk about snooping on your kids online really applies to younger kids—middle schoolers, high schoolers, and college-aged kids. After your kids get a bit older and a lot more mature, your online relationship with them changes—or should change, anyway.

As your children move away from home and establish families of their own, finding the time to talk is a major challenge. Days, weeks, or even months might go by where neither of you can find the time to phone. Here is where Facebook can be of real value.

When you add a grown child to your Facebook friends list, that child now is privy to all the status updates you make—and vice versa. This is a great way to keep each other informed of all the little things happening in your lives.

For more detailed information, take advantage of Facebook's private messaging system. This

Note

Learn more about sending and receiving private messages in Chapter 9, "Exchanging Private Messages."

is like email for Facebookers, where you use Facebook to send longer messages back and forth. It's not quite the same as exchanging written letters, but it's better than not writing at all.

Note

Learn more about instant messaging in Chapter 10, "Chatting with Family and Friends—Live."

And if you both happen to find yourself online at the same time (check the chat list on your Home page), you can use Facebook's chat feature to instant message in real time with your child. It's almost like talking in person!

Tracking Personal Info

The obvious thing to look at when you're snooping on (excuse me, observing) your child on Facebook is his status updates. These tell you what he's doing and thinking about at the moment.

But you also want to pay attention to the personal information he supplies to the Facebook site, in particular what's on the Info tab on his Profile page. There are a number of things to look for here.

First, it's always fun to observe your child's relationship status. Trust me; this might be the first place you learn that he's gotten a new girlfriend or broken up with his old one.

I also like to look at what the kid is watching and listening to these days. An odd change in listening habits, for example, might signal other changes in behavior. It's not a perfect indicator, by any means, but you can get a sense of how a child is leaning by the music he listens to and the movies he watches.

Finally, take a look at the contact information at the bottom of the Info tab. If there's any information there at all, it's time to break your cover and have a talk with your child. Your child should not, under any circumstances, publicly list his phone number, mailing address, or email address. There should be no way for bad guys to contact your kids online, which means keeping all this contact information private. It's worth a few temporary bad feelings to keep your kids from putting too much of themselves online—and potentially putting themselves in harm's way.

Chapter 7

Organizing Groups of Friends

After you've been on Facebook for any length of time, you find that you've added quite a few people to your friends list. Between old friends from your youth, current friends and coworkers, and assorted family members, you might end up with anywhere from a few dozen to a few hundred Facebook friends. Good for you!

The problem with having so many friends on Facebook, however, is managing them. That's a lot of people to track in your News Feed, for example. It's also difficult to find that one individual friend you want to email or send a photo to; when you have an ever expanding friends list, locating one single friend is a little like finding a needle in a haystack.

How, then, do you better manage your Facebook friends? You do so by organizing your friends into separate friends lists, as you learn next.

Working with Friends Lists

One of the big problems with Facebook is that you pretty much share everything with everyone. (A social network is all about sharing stuff publicly, after all.) That's fine for some folks, but others like to live their online life in a bit more compartmentalized fashion.

When it comes to managing large lists of friends, then, the key is to create *custom* lists within your main list. A Facebook list is simply a subset of your total friends list, organized however you want. It isn't something that your friends have to join; there's really no two-way participation. It's merely a way to send posts, photos, chats, and other files to selected friends only, instead of your entire friends list. And it's a great way to simplify your News Feed, by viewing only posts from specific lists of friends.

In terms of what kinds of lists to create, you might want to create a list that contains only family members. Or you could create a list of people you currently work with. You can also create a list for people on your son's soccer team or in your daughter's ballet class. You can create a list for your book club, church group, or community group. You can even create lists for collaborative projects, such as for a class or business project.

When you have a custom list (or two or three), it's easy enough to find individuals on that list, or to send messages to all the members of the list. It's a lot easier to manage small lists of friends than it is to deal with all your friends at once.

For example, you might make one post with photos from the latest family gathering, another post talking about the wild party you attended over the weekend, and a third post commenting on some work-related issue. It helps keep your various social lives separate.

Viewing Your Lists

The lists that you and Facebook create are displayed in the Lists section of the left sidebar on the Facebook Home page, as shown in Figure 7.1. If you have more lists than can fit in this space, hover over the Lists header and click More to view the rest on a separate Lists page.

Figure 7.1. *The Lists section on your Facebook Home page.*

Figure 7.2 shows Facebook's Lists page. Click the name of any list to view posts from members of this list.

Figure 7.2. *Viewing your lists.*

Understanding Facebook's Smart Lists

To help you get started with friends lists, Facebook creates a handful of automatic lists for you, which it calls *smart lists*. You can use these smart lists if you like, or ignore them and create your own custom lists.

What smart lists does Facebook create for you? You'll see three by default:

- **Close Friends**, meant to host your closest real-world friends.
- **Acquaintances**, meant for those friends who aren't really close friends.
- **Family**, for your relatives.

In addition, Facebook may create smart lists based on your work, school, and local affiliations. For example, if you work at General Motors, you might see a General Motors list, pre-populated with other GM workers you count as Facebook friends. If you went to Indiana University, you might find an IU list filled with other Hoosier alumni on your friends list. Or if you live in San Diego, don't be surprised to see a list filled with your San Diego friends.

> **! Caution**
>
> Be careful about putting too many people into your Close Friends list. By default, Facebook notifies you every time someone on this list posts a new status update.

Creating a New Friends List

To get the most out of Facebook's friends lists, you'll want to create your own custom lists. It's easy to do:

1. From Facebook's Home page, hover over the Lists header in the sidebar, and click More.

2. When the Lists page appears, click the Create a List button at the top of the page.

3. When the Create a List dialog box appears, as shown in Figure 7.3, enter a name for this list, and then click the Create List button.

Figure 7.3. *Creating a new list.*

Facebook now displays the page for this new list. At this point you can add friends to the list, as described next.

Adding Friends to a List

There are two ways to add friends to a smart list or a list that you've created.

First, you can go to a friend's Profile page and hover over the Friends button. This displays a pop-up menu of all your lists, as shown in Figure 7.4; check those lists you want this friend in.

Note

A friend can be in more than one of your lists.

Figure 7.4. *Adding a friend to a list from his Profile page.*

You can also add friends to a list from that list's page. Here's how it works:

1. From Facebook's Home page, hover over the Lists header in the sidebar, and click More.

2. When the Lists page appears, click the link for the list you want to edit.

3. When the list page appears, as shown in Figure 7.5, you see a list of suggested friends in the right column. To add one of these folks to the list, click the Add button.

Figure 7.5. *Adding friends to a list from the list page.*

4. To add other friends to this list, enter their names into the Add Friends to This List box at the top right. Matching friends will appear in a drop-down list; click a friend to add him or her to your list.

Reading Posts from a List

One of the benefits of friends lists is making it easy to read those updates you care most about. For example, you can choose to read only posts from family members, and thus ignore those posts from your legion of non-family friends.

Tip

To remove a friend from a list, go to the list page, click the Manage List button, and select Add/Remove Friends. When the next dialog box appears, find the friend you want to delete, and click that person's thumbnail to remove the check box.

To read posts from the members of a given list, simply click the name of that list in the Lists section of your Facebook Home page. This displays the list page, like the one shown in Figure 7.6. This page displays a news feed of updates from list members and only list members.

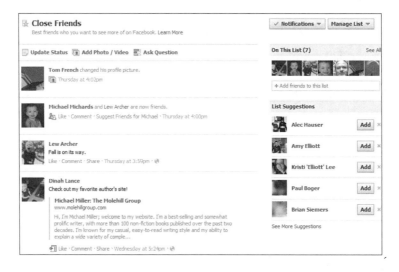

Figure 7.6. *Reading posts on a list page.*

Posting to a List

Here's another neat aspect of Facebook's friends list. When you post a new status update, you can opt to post only to members of a given list. We'll discuss this in more depth in Chapter 8, "Updating Your Friends on What You've Been Doing." Turn there to learn more.

Getting Rid of Unwanted Friends

While we're on the topic of managing your Facebook friends, what do you do about those friends who you really don't want to be friends with anymore? Maybe it's someone who's fallen off your radar, a coworker who changed jobs, an acquaintance who's proven more annoying than friendly, or a black sheep family member you'd prefer to disown. Do you need to keep these people on your friends list forever?

The answer, of course, is that you don't. You can, at any time, remove any individual from your Facebook friends list. This is called *unfriending* the person, and it happens all the time. In fact, the person you unfriend doesn't even know he's been ditched; you just get rid of him and that's that.

Here's how to do it:

1. Click your name in the Facebook toolbar.
2. When your Profile page appears, click the Friends graphic.
3. When the Friends page appears, click the friend you want to remove.
4. When that friend's Profile page appears, hover over the Friends button, and select Unfriend from the pop-up menu.
5. When prompted if you want to remove that person as a friend, click the Remove from Friends button.

That's it. The person is no longer your official Facebook friend.

Blocking Unwanted Users

Just because you remove someone as your friend doesn't mean that you become invisible to that person on Facebook. That person can still message you and, unless you alter your privacy settings, view certain content on your Profile page.

If you think that someone is acting like a stalker, it might be best to completely block all contact from that person. You do this by adding this individual to what Facebook calls your

Note

You can, at any time, re-add an unfriended person as a friend. You just have to go through the whole invite-a-friend process again, no big deal.

block list. Individuals on this list cannot view your Profile page, send you private messages, or even find you in search of the Facebook site. It's a great way to shield yourself from online stalkers—or just people you never want to hear from again.

Learn more about determining who can and can't view your personal information in Chapter 15, "Keeping Some Things Private: Managing Facebook's Privacy Settings."

To block someone in this fashion, follow these steps:

1. Click the down arrow on the Facebook toolbar, and then click Privacy Settings.

2. When the Privacy Settings page appears, go to the Manage People and Apps section at the bottom of the page, and click Manage Blocking.

3. When the Managing Blocking page appears, as shown in Figure 7.7, go to the Block Users section, and enter that person's Facebook name into the Name box or enter her email address into the Email box.

Figure 7.7. *Adding someone to your block list.*

4. Click the appropriate Block button.

People you've blocked are now listed on the Managing Blocking page. To unblock a given individual, click the Unblock link next to her name.

How Many Friends Is Too Many?

Younger Facebook users tend to have more friends than do older users. I'm not quite sure why this is the case; after all, we've met a lot more people in our years than younger users have in their limited time walking this planet.

Still, younger folks are more likely to use Facebook as the hub for all their social interactions, and thus have lots of people on their friends list who they barely know, if they know them at all. Those of our generation, being older, wiser, and more discriminate, tend to avoid friending mere acquaintances. Our friends lists are more likely to contain real friends.

That said, it's easy to build up a Facebook friends list that registers in the triple digits. I don't care how gregarious you are, it's unlikely that you have that many true friends. Really, take a look at your list—how many people on there really belong?

Because we tend to accumulate Facebook friends much the same way as our yards accumulate dandelions, from time to time you might want to cull the pretenders from your list of friends. Does that neighbor two streets over really need to be there? Or the checkout lady from the supermarket? Or for that matter, weird cousin Ernie?

Sometimes who you let on your friends list is a matter of strategy. Take, for example, my stepdaughter, who is a nurse at a major metropolitan hospital. Her policy is to allow other nurses on her friends list but not doctors or hospital administrators. To her thinking, her coworkers—people at her level—can be friends, but her bosses can't. Makes sense to me.

You might want to develop similar strategies for deciding who you do or don't let onto your friends list. Maybe it's as simple as saying anyone who gets a Christmas card (or you get a Christmas card from) gets on the list. Or only those people you talk or write to once a year get on the list. Or people who work in your department, but not those who work in remote offices. You get to make the rules.

The point is that even though Facebook is a social network, you don't have to network with everyone on the site. You can pick and choose those people you befriend—and sometimes a smaller circle of friends is better.

Chapter 8

Updating Your Friends on What You're Doing

We've talked a lot about Facebook being the perfect place to update your friends and family on what you're up to—things you're doing, thoughts you're thinking, accomplishments you're accomplishing, you name it. The easiest way to let people know what's what is to post what Facebook calls a *status update*.

Every status update you make is broadcast to everyone on your friends list, displayed in the News Feed on their Home pages. This way everyone who cares enough about you to make you a friend knows everything you post about. And that can be quite a lot—from simple text posts to photos and videos and even links to other web pages.

What Is a Status Update?

Quite literally, a Facebook status update is an update of your status. Yeah, that's self-defining, but in essence it's a way to describe what you're doing or thinking about at the moment. It's a snapshot into your life, posted as a short text on the Facebook site.

A status update is, at its most basic, a brief text message. It can be as short as a word or two, or it can be several paragraphs long; that's up to you. (The official maximum limit is 5,000 characters, which should do for most folks.)

Although a basic status update is all text, you can also attach various multimedia elements to your status updates, including digital photographs, videos, questions, and links to other web pages. You can also "tag" other Facebook users and groups in your updates, so that their names appear as clickable links (to their Profile pages, of course).

The nice thing about a status update is that it's a post-once, read-many process. That is, a single status update is broadcast to all the people on your friends list. If you have 100 friends, that's 100 people that read the single status update you posted.

Note

Various Facebook applications also let you attach application-specific items to your status updates. Learn more about these applications in Chapter 20, "Finding Fun Games and Applications."

You can also target your status updates to specific friends lists. As you learned in the previous chapter, Facebook lets you organize your friends into different lists; when you post a status update, you can select which list of friends to send it to—or to send it to all your Facebook friends.

Status updates appear in multiple places on the Facebook site. First, your status updates appear on your own Profile page, newest at the top. More important, your status updates also appear on your friends' Home pages, in their News Feeds, as shown in Figure 8.1. This way your friends are kept updated as to what you're doing and thinking.

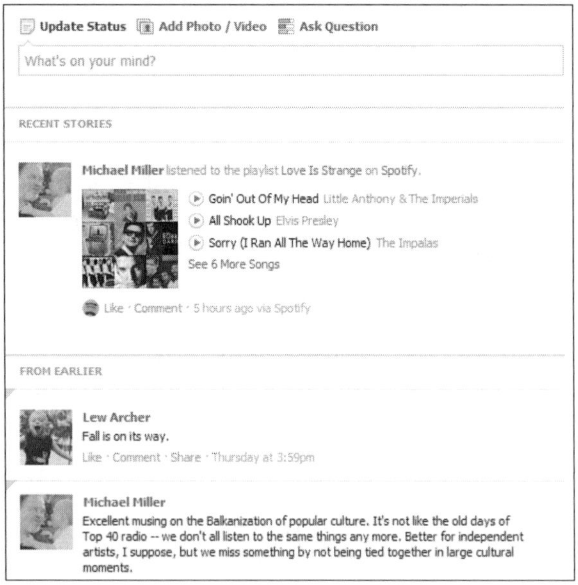

📝 Update Status   📷 Add Photo / Video   ☰ Ask Question

What's on your mind?

RECENT STORIES

Michael Miller listened to the playlist Love Is Strange on Spotify.

▶ **Goin' Out Of My Head** Little Anthony & The Imperials
▶ **All Shook Up** Elvis Presley
▶ **Sorry (I Ran All The Way Home)** The Impalas
See 6 More Songs

👍 Like · Comment · 5 hours ago via Spotify

FROM EARLIER

Lew Archer
Fall is on its way.
Like · Comment · Share · Thursday at 3:59pm

Michael Miller
Excellent musing on the Balkanization of popular culture. It's not like the old days of Top 40 radio -- we don't all listen to the same things any more. Better for independent artists, I suppose, but we miss something by not being tied together in large cultural moments.

Figure 8.1. *Status updates on a friends' Home page.*

Where to Update Your Status

When you want to update your status, there are two different places you can do it.

First, you can go to your Home page, at the top of which resides the box you see in Figure 8.2. This box, which initially has the words "What's on your mind?" inside, is officially called the *Publisher box*. This box is one place to enter your updates; click the Share button to post a new status update.

Figure 8.2. *The Publisher box at the top of your Home page.*

You can also find a Publisher box on your own Profile page. As you can see in Figure 8.3, it's pretty much the same box, but with a few extra icons for posting updates to your work and education, family and relationships, living, health and wellness, and milestones and experiences.

Figure 8.3. *The Publisher box on your Profile page.*

By the way, you can also post status updates from your mobile phone, as a standard text message. Or if you have a Facebook application for your iPhone or other smartphone, you can use that app to post your updates.

Caution

Do not confuse these Publisher boxes with the similar box found at the top of your *friends'* Profile pages. The box on a friend's page is used to post a message to that friend on that friend's Profile page only. What you post on a friend's page is *not* a regular status update and does not make it into anyone else's News Feed.

How to Update Your Status

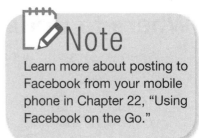

Note

Learn more about posting to Facebook from your mobile phone in Chapter 22, "Using Facebook on the Go."

Posting a status update is a relatively simple procedure. It can get a little more complicated, however, if you choose to attach a photo, video, question, or web link to the basic text message.

Posting a Simple Text Update

Understandably, Facebook makes it extremely easy to post a status update. You have to be signed into Facebook, of course, but then you follow these simple steps:

1. Navigate to the Facebook Home page or your personal Profile page, and go to the Publisher box.

2. If it's not already selected, click Update Status.

3. Type your message into the What's on Your Mind? box. As you do this, the box expands, as shown in Figure 8.4.

Figure 8.4. *Entering a status update.*

4. If you're with someone else and want to mention them in the post, click the Who Are You With? button on the bottom left and enter that person's name.

5. If you want to include your current location in your post, click the Where Are You? button (second from the left) and enter the city or place where you are.

6. To determine who can read this post, click the second blue button from the right (Public, by default), and make a selection. As you can see in Figure 8.5, you can opt to make the post Public (anyone who's subscribed to your posts can read it), visible only to your Friends, or Custom. (You select individuals who can and can't view it.) Alternatively, you can select which friends list can view the update.

Figure 8.5. *Selecting who can view a post.*

7. When you're ready to post your update, click the Post button.

Attaching a Photo or Video

So far, so good. But what if you'd like to attach a photo or video to a status update? You can, you know; it's a great way to share a special photo with your friends, without them having to navigate to and through your photo albums. In this instance, you follow these steps:

Note

Any additions you make to your Facebook photo albums are automatically posted as status updates. Any single picture you post with a status update is automatically added to your Wall Photos album. (Unless you posted it from your mobile phone, in which case it ends up in the Mobile Uploads album.)

1. Go to the Publisher box on your Home or Profile page, and click Add Photo/Video.

2. This expands the Publisher box, as shown in Figure 8.6. To attach a photo or video from your computer, click Upload Photo/Video. When the panel changes, click the Browse or Choose Button; when the Open dialog box appears, navigate to and select the file you want, and then click the Open button.

Figure 8.6. *Getting ready to attach a photo to a status update.*

3. To attach a new photo or video taken with your computer's webcam, click the Use Webcam link. When the panel changes to display your live webcam, as shown in Figure 8.7, click the red Record button to record a video. To take a still picture, click the Switch to Photo button on the top right and proceed from there.

Figure 8.7. *Using your webcam to create a photo or video for a status post.*

4. To create a new photo album and upload multiple photos, click Create Photo Album. When the Upload Photos dialog box appears, click the Select Photos button. When the Open dialog box appears, navigate to and select the photos you want to upload, and then click the Open button. When the Upload Photos dialog box reappears, enter a name and location for your album, select whether you're uploading at standard or high resolution, and then click the Create Album button.

Note

Learn more about uploading photos to Facebook in Chapter 11, "Sharing Family Pictures."

5. Click the Post button to post your photo(s) or video.

Attaching a Link to Another Web Page

Here's something else you can add to a status update—a link to a particular web page or article you like. Not only does Facebook add a link to the specified page, it also lets you include a thumbnail image from that page with the status update.

Here's how it works:

1. From the Publisher box, click Status Update.

2. Enter your update as normal, and include the URL for the page you want to link to.

3. Facebook should recognize the link and display a Link panel, as shown in Figure 8.8. Select a thumbnail image from the web page to accompany the link, or check the No Thumbnail box.

4. Complete the rest of your post as normal, including selecting who can view the post.

5. Click the Post button.

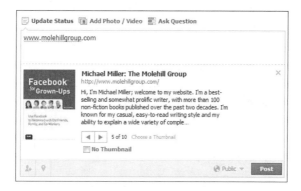

Figure 8.8. *Adding a web link to a status update.*

Asking a Question

Facebook also lets you ask questions of the people on your friends list. You can use this to gather opinions, recommendations, and the like. Here's how it works:

1. Click Ask Question above the Publisher box.

2. When the Question panel appears, as shown in Figure 8.8, enter your question into the Ask Something box.

3. Select who can view this post.

4. Click the Post button.

Figure 8.9. *Asking a question of your Facebook friends.*

When the question appears in your friends' News Feeds, as shown in Figure 8.10, they can answer the question by filling in the blank and clicking the Add button. The "live" answers to your question are shown on your own Profile page; as you can see in Figure 8.11, you can get a visual feel on how many people (and whom) supplied which answers.

Figure 8.10. *Answering a friend's question.*

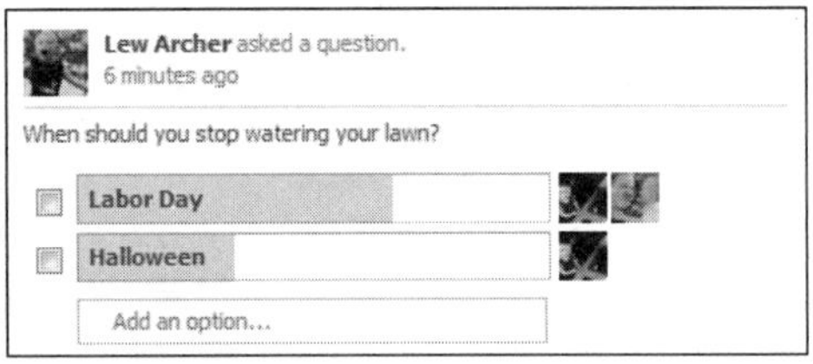

Figure 8.11. *Viewing answers to a question.*

Tagging a Friend in a Post

Sometimes you might want to mention one of your friends in a status update. Or maybe you want to include a shout out to one of the Facebook groups to which you belong. Well, there's a way to "tag" friends and groups in your status updates so that the update includes a link to the tagged person or group, as shown in Figure 8.12.

Figure 8.12. *A status update "tagged" with a clickable link to a particular person on the Facebook site.*

To tag a person or group in a status update, simply begin to type that person's name in the Publisher box. As you type, Facebook displays a drop-down list with matching entries, as shown in Figure 8.13; select the friend or group from the list, and then continue typing the rest of your update as normal.

Note

Facebook lets you tag friends, groups, fan pages, events, and applications.

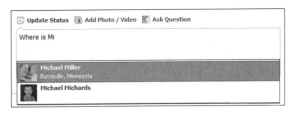

Figure 8.13. *Tagging a friend in a status update.*

Anyone reading this status update sees the tagged entity as a blue text link. Clicking the link displays the Facebook page for the person or item you tagged.

Tip

If you change your mind about a status update you've made, you can delete that post from Facebook. Go to your Profile page, and scroll to the post you want to delete. Click the Edit or Remove (Pencil) button and select Delete Post. When the Delete post dialog box appears, click the Remove Post button.

Deciding What to Write About

When it comes to writing a status update, what qualifies as something worthwhile to post about? Unfortunately—and I really mean that— there are no rules or guidelines as to what's acceptable and what's not. So you run into a lot of useless drivel in your News Feed, along with useful updates and the occasional gem of an observation.

Let me demonstrate, by listing a random sampling of status updates culled from my own News Feed. These are actual updates from my actual friends, although some of the details have been changed to protect the innocent.

marriages rise + fall on communication. come to think of it, all relationships do. things to consider: tone, timing, and trust.

Must enjoy summer while we still can!

i just sneezed all over my laptop screen. yuck.

A shout-out to my BFAM, who is being interviewed on NPR, right this very minute, about his new book

"The stiffest tree is most easily cracked, while the bamboo or willow survives by bending with the wind" - Bruce Lee

A friend posted this today and I love it, so I am re-posting -- words to live by: If you are honest, people may cheat you. Be honest anyway. If you find happiness, people may be jealous. Be happy anyway. The good you do today may be forgotten tomorrow. Do good anyway. Give the world the best you have and it may never be enough. Give your best anyway. For you see, in the end, it is between you and God. It was never between you and them anyway

Some people feel threatened by others who are recovering alcoholics.

It's a good day

pathetic excuse for a day...

What say we head over to the coast and listen to a little Western music?

Have you tried 4G? Do you think it is faster?

Wonderful time in Chicago so far. Many reunions and much laughter.

whining because husband took the car today, and of course, suddenly, she just HAS to go to Bed, Bath and Beyond to buy new sheets. It simply cannot wait another day!

Off to the Illinois State Fair with Jackson to see Sheila Simon's band, Loose Gravel and eat some corndogs. No pix please.

Our a/c has not turned off all day. It is raining, but it is still 90+F.

Thanks to the Gods of Caffeine and Sugar, without whom I'd be unable to function.

So...24 years of marriage has literally flown by! I have a wonderful husband and partner on this journey.

In Vermont, It is illegal for women to wear false teeth without the written permission of their husbands.

(Jane Smith) doesn't trust cephalopods, and neither should you.

And these are just the text-only updates; you also find a ton of photos, videos, links, and the rest in your News Feed.

Take a look at these posts and note the variable grammar, spelling, and punctuation used; I'll discuss this in the following section. But beyond that, observe the variety of what people think is noteworthy. There are interesting observations, heartfelt tributes, funny quotations, petty complaints, and mundane statements of activity. In short, you can post pretty much anything you want and you won't get a lot of complaints.

That said, I can probably do without the more mundane observations. ("I just sneezed all over my laptop screen.") I don't need to know when you woke up, when you ate lunch, when you're going to sleep, and that sort of thing. Maybe some people care, but most don't.

It's better if you post on more interesting and unique topics. The fact that you went to a concert or read a book is interesting; it's even more interesting than what you thought about it.

Also interesting are major life events, such as anniversaries, graduations, and such. Some thoughts from some people are interesting; other thoughts from other people aren't. Some posts are funny; some are poignant; some are just silly. Some are simply factual; some speculate. Some are intimate, embarrassingly so. And a lot are self-centered; if you don't know the person, you might not care at all.

My point, then, is that there often is no point in what you post. You're updating your status, after all, and what's important to you might not be important to your friends. Try to keep a handle on that and post about stuff your Facebook friends might be interested in. If you go too far outside, you might find your posts dropped from your friends' News Feeds, or even worse, get yourself unfriended. Not everyone cares about what you care about, after all; what you find interesting might not be interesting at all to anyone else.

Employing "Facebook Grammar"

Writing a Facebook status update is a bit like sending a text message on your cell phone. You do it quickly, without a lot of preparation beforehand or editing afterward. It's an in-the-moment communication, and as such, you can't be expected to take the time to create a grammatically perfect message.

As such, status updates do not have to—and seldom do—conform to proper grammar, spelling, and sentence structure. It's common to abbreviate longer words, use familiar acronyms, substitute single letters and numbers for whole words, and refrain from all punctuation.

For example, if you're posting about seeing your peeps (that's Facebook for "people") on Friday, instead of writing "I'll see you on Friday," you might post "C U Fri." You could even forgo capitalization and post "cu fri." Facebookers, especially more seasoned ones, know what you're talking about.

Note

It's also acceptable, at least to some users, to have the occasional misspelling. It's not something I personally like to do or see, but I'm a professional writer and pickier about these things; most people let it slide if you get the spelling wrong once in a while.

To that end, you can use many of the same acronyms that have been used for decades in text messaging, instant messaging, and Internet chat rooms. Given that you're not a hip, young communicator like your kids probably are, you might not be familiar with all these online shortcuts. For your edification, then, I've assembled a short list of the most popular of these acronyms, which you find in Table 8.1. Use them wisely.

Table 8.1 Common Facebook Acronyms

Acronym	Description
AFAIK	As far as I know
ASAP	As soon as possible
ASL	Age/sex/location
B/W	Between
B4	Before
BC	Because
BFN	Bye for now
BR	Best regards
BRB	Be right back
BTW	By the way
CU	See you
Cuz	Because
FB	Facebook
FTF	Face to face
FWIW	For what it's worth
FYI	For your information
GM	Good morning
GN	Good night
HTH	Hope that helps
IDK	I don't know
IM	Instant message
IMHO	In my humble opinion
IRL	In real life
JK	Just kidding
K	Okay
L8	Late
L8r	Later
LMAO	Laughing my ass off

Acronym	Description
LMK	Let me know
LOL	Laughing out loud
NSFW	Not safe for work
OH	Overheard
OMG	Oh my God
Pls or Plz	Please
Ppl or peeps	People
R	Are
Rly	Really
ROFL	Rolling on the floor laughing
SD	Sweet dreams
Tht	That
Thx or Tnx	Thanks
TY	Thank you
TTYL	Talk to you later
U	You
Ur	Your
WTF	What the f**k
WTH	What the hell
YMMV	Your mileage may vary
YW	You're welcome
Zzz	Sleeping

Armed with these helpful shortcuts, U should be able to FB with all the young ppl. Of course, YMMV. BFN.

How Often Is Enough?

How often should you update your Facebook status? That's an interesting question, without a defined answer.

Some of my Facebook friends post frequently—several times a day. Some post only occasionally, once a month or so. Most, however, post once a day or once every few days. So if there's an average, that's it.

Some of the more frequent posters are justified, in that they post a lot of useful information. For example, I'm particularly fond of film critic Roger Ebert's Facebook posts; even though he posts every few hours, each post is informative and entertaining—well worth reading.

Other frequent posters I find more annoying. These folks' posts are often more personal and less useful; every little tic and burp is immortalized in its own update. That's probably posting too much.

On the other hand, my friends who only post once a month or so probably aren't trying hard enough. I'd like to hear from them more often; certainly they're doing something interesting that's worth posting about. After a while, I tend to forget that they're still around.

So you need to post often enough that your friends don't forget about you, but not so often that they wish you'd just shut up. I suppose your update frequency has something to do with what it is you're doing and how interesting that is. But it's okay to post just to let people know you're still there—as long as you don't do so hourly.

Chapter 9

Exchanging Private Messages

The whole goal of Facebook and social networking is to... well, to network *socially*. And in this context, socially means publicly, which is where we get Facebook's very public status updates, Wall postings, and the like.

But what if you see an old friend online and want to drop a more private note? What if you have something to say that you don't want the whole world to see? Do all your Facebook communications have to be public ones?

The answer, of course, is no; Facebook doesn't force you into all-public communication. There's a way to send private messages on Facebook, which is how you establish more personal relationships with your friends.

Understanding Facebook's Messages System

It's not that Facebook doesn't like private messages between its users. It's that the Facebook community grows and benefits when communication is more public. A public status update or Wall posting goes into the Facebook system, where it's searchable and viewable by others, which leads to more connections and more communication. (It also helps Facebook target its ads to you, but that's another story—or is it?)

Despite its preference for public communication, Facebook does provide a couple of different methods for private communication. As you learn in the next chapter, Facebook offers an instant messaging service for real-time communication between users. It also offers more traditional private messaging and email, which is what we're discussing here.

Until recently, all these messaging features functioned independently; you didn't mix email messages with Wall postings or chats. But that changed when Facebook instituted its new Messages feature, which consolidates all private messages in a single place.

Messages is the central hub for all your private messaging on the Facebook network. Every private communication you receive or take part in is archived here—private messages from your Facebook friends, chat sessions, even emails sent to your @facebook.com address (which I discuss in a moment). These messages, no matter the type, are organized by sender, so you can view all your communications with specific friends at a glance.

Messages also lets you easily send messages to Facebook friends. You have the choice of sending messages via Facebook private message, Facebook chat, email, or SMS mobile phone text messaging. With Messages, it's the message that's important, not the medium.

Because Messages sorts all communications by user, you create an ongoing archive of all your conversations with each of your friends. It's a lifelong conversational history, so you always know what you've talked about, even when your memory fails you.

Using Facebook's Email System

One important feature of Facebook's new Messages system is that every Facebook member now has her own @facebook.com email address. This is a private email address that's linked to your Facebook username and account; your email address is your Facebook username followed by @facebook.com, like this: *username*@facebook.com.

Understanding Facebook's Email

Having your own Facebook email address makes it easy to communicate not only with other Facebook members, but also with users outside of Facebook. Your Facebook friends see your email messages just like private

Facebook messages, with no subject lines, cc's, or the like; non-Facebook users see traditional-looking email messages.

Facebook's new email system also simplifies things when you're sending emails. You don't have to enter a subject line, you can't cc or bcc anyone on your messages, and you don't have to click a Send button; the message is sent when you press the Enter key on your computer keyboard.

The email messages you see in Messages look more like Facebook's other private messages, which I promise we get to in a moment. Individual emails are organized into "conversations" by sender, so you have all your messages from one person in a single place. There are no folders or subfolders for organizing your messages.

Facebook email, then, presents a different metaphor than that employed by traditional email programs and services. Messages isn't like Microsoft Outlook or even Gmail; you get your messages Facebook's way (organized by user), with no other options available. Like I said, it's different, but it seems to fit well within the Facebook universe.

What a @facebook.com email address does is let people who aren't Facebook members communicate with you via Facebook. If you spend your entire waking life inside the Facebook interface, you can now receive messages from your non-Facebook friends. All you have to do is provide them with your new @facebook.com email address, and you receive their emails from within Facebook in the new Messages center. It makes the site a one-stop messaging shop for diehard Facebook users.

Claiming Your Email Address

Unfortunately, Facebook doesn't assign email addresses automatically; you have to request it manually. To do so, follow these steps:

1. Go to your Facebook Home page, and click Messages in the sidebar.

2. When the Messages page appears, click the Claim Your Facebook Email link at the top of the page. (This link disappears after you claim your address.)

3. When the pop-up pane appears, as shown in Figure 9.1, select one of the suggested email addresses or enter your own choice into the empty box.

4. Click the Activate Email button.

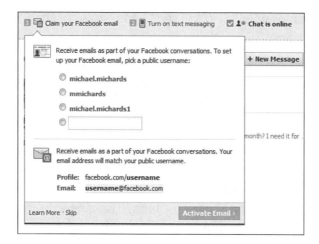

Figure 9.1. *Selecting your Facebook email address.*

Reading Your Messages

Let's start by visiting Facebook's Messages center to read messages you've received from others. As you can see in Figure 9.2, new messages are highlighted on and accessed from the Messages button on the Facebook toolbar. If you supplied your mobile phone number, you are also notified of new messages (including Wall postings) via text messaging. (This feature can be disabled, however, if you find this kind of thing annoying.)

Figure 9.2. *New messages are highlighted on the Messages button on the Facebook toolbar.*

You open the Messages page itself by clicking Messages in the sidebar on your Facebook home page. As you can see in Figure 9.3, this page displays all the messages and communications you've received across the Facebook site. Messages are listed in reverse chronological order, newest first. There's no distinction for type of message; emails look the same as private messages or chat sessions. Unread messages are shaded in blue.

Figure 9.3. *Facebook's new Messages page; all communications are listed, no matter the type.*

The type of message sent or received is indicated by an icon on the far right side of the message list, beside the time/date indicator. An Envelope icon indicates an email message; a Word Balloon icon indicates a chat or instant message; a Phone icon indicates a text message; and no icon means you got a private message from a Facebook friend.

To view a message, simply click it. The resulting page lists all messages to and from that person, in the form of a flowing conversation. On this page, the newest messages are at the bottom. (That's odd, I know, considering on all other Facebook pages the newest messages are at the top. Oh well; Facebook has never been known for interface consistency.)

To send another message to this person, simply enter your message into the text box at the bottom of the page, and click Reply or press Enter. That's pretty easy.

Note

Not all messages are displayed on the main Messages page; you see only messages from Facebook members, not messages sent via email from outsiders. Click Other in the Messages section of the sidebar to display email messages sent from non-Facebook members, as well as messages and invitations from pages to which you've subscribed.

Figure 9.4. *Viewing messages to and from a specific friend.*

Sending a Private Message or Email

It's just as easy to send a new message. You can send a message to a Facebook friend (by entering that friend's name) or to anyone outside the Facebook system (by entering that person's email address).

Follow these steps:

1. From the Messages page, click the New Message button.

2. When the New Message dialog box appears, as shown in Figure 9.5, enter the Facebook name or non-Facebook email address of the recipient into the To box.

3. Enter your message into the Message box.

4. To attach a file to this message, click the Paperclip icon. This opens the Open dialog box; navigate to and select the file you want to attach, and then click the Open button.

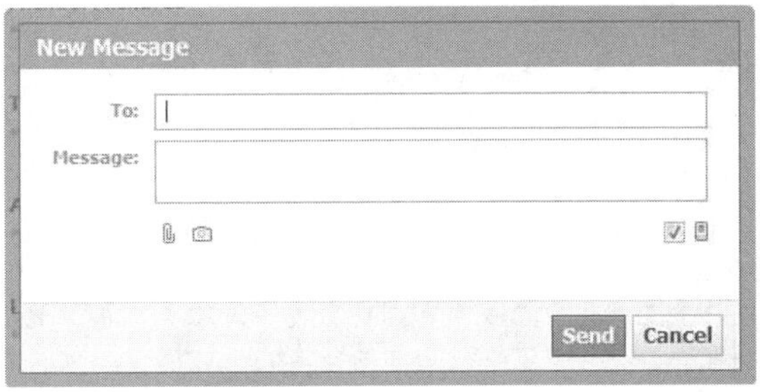

Figure 9.5. *Sending a new private message via Facebook Messages.*

5. To attach a picture of video to this message, click the Camera icon. This opens the Open dialog box; navigate to and select the file you want to attach, and then click the Open button.

6. Press Enter, or click the Send button to send the message on its way.

By default, messages are sent via Facebook's messaging system to Facebook users or via normal email for non-Facebook recipients. If you'd rather the recipient also receive the message on his mobile phone, check the Also Send as Text Message option (in the right corner of the dialog box) before you send it on its way.

Facebook Email?

So Facebook gives you your own facebook.com email address. Is it something you're likely to use?

Probably not—and here's why.

If someone is already on Facebook, she can contact you via Facebook's built-in messaging system, she can post on your Wall; heck, she can even chat you up in a text or video chat. She doesn't need to email you.

The only time someone would send email to your facebook.com address is if they're not on Facebook. Given that most of your friends are likely to be on Facebook, and those that aren't probably have your regular email address, the facebook.com email address is somewhat pointless.

Still, I appreciate Facebook providing the facebook.com address. It fits into Facebook's goal of being your single gateway for all online communication and activity. I mean, if you're going to rule the world, you better have your own email system, right?

So Facebook provides members with their own facebook.com addresses with the hope that all their non-Facebook friends will use it to communicate with them. And when they do, of course, that's an opportunity to both capture non-Facebook communications and try to entice non-Facebookers to join the community. Certainly, there's no downside to Facebook for doing so.

Chapter 10

Chatting with Family and Friends—Live

In the previous chapter, we discussed one way to communicate privately with family and friends online, via Facebook's Messages or email system. Communicating via email can be slow, however, especially if the person you're writing to doesn't check her messages all that often.

If you want a more immediate means of communication, check out Facebook's live chat feature. This lets you communicate in real time with your friends, using one-to-one text messages. Like email messages, these are totally private communications; no one but you and the person you're talking to can read them.

In addition, Facebook now offers a *video* chat feature, which is great for just sitting back and talking to friends and family. What could be easier?

What's Chat—and Who Uses It?

Okay, so here's the deal. What Facebook calls "chat," everybody else in the world calls *instant messaging*. You might or might not be familiar with instant messaging (or what those in the know call IM), but I guarantee your kids know what it is.

Understanding Instant Messaging

Instant messaging is like text messaging with your computer instead of your phone, and it's widely used by the younger generation. In fact, I'd bet big numbers that your kids already use instant messaging of one flavor or another.

And there are several flavors of instant messaging—that is, several different IM services. The most popular of these are Yahoo! Messenger (YM), AOL Instant Messenger (AIM), ICQ, Google Talk, Windows Live Messenger, and Skype. In general, these IM services don't talk to each other; you can only talk to other people who use the same service you do.

In reality, most younger users subscribe to more than one IM service. (All of them are free to use.) YM and AIM are the two most popular freestanding IM services, especially with those in their teens and twenties. It's common to find both YM and AIM windows open on a kid's computer with multiple conversations taking place between your kid and a dozen or so of her friends.

Note

Skype is best known for its Internet-based telephone service but also offers instant messaging between users. It also offers video chat—and powers Facebook's video chat services. Read the "Integrating Facebook with Skype" section later in this chapter to learn more.

Welcome to Facebook Chat

Facebook's chat works just like these more traditional IM services but is exclusive to Facebook users. It runs within your web browser only when you're logged into the Facebook site; it's well integrated with the Facebook interface.

Note

If you happen to subscribe to the AIM service, you can talk to your Facebook friends directly from the AIM program window.

As such, Facebook chat lets you carry on real-time conversations with any of your Facebook friends who are also logged onto the site. Obviously, you can't talk with someone who isn't logged on. But as long as a friend is online in Facebook at the same time you are, you can chat to your heart's delight.

Chatting, by the way, consists of sending and receiving sequential text messages to and from your friend. It's not a video chat, and there's no audio involved (although Facebook does offer video chat, which I discuss a bit later in this chapter); Facebook's chat feature is a text-only thing. It's pretty much like sending and receiving one text message after another on your cell phone, except that the entire thread of the conversation appears in a single chat window—which makes it easier to keep track of who's saying what.

Knowing this, you shouldn't get Facebook chat confused with web-based chat rooms. (And if you don't know what a chat room is, ask your kids.) Despite the similar names, Facebook chat is purely a one-to-one conversation; you can't have a multiple-person chat, as you can in a chat room on another site. A Facebook chat is between you and a single friend only.

That said, you can conduct multiple chats at the same time. That is, you can have one chat window open to talk with your friend John, another to chat with your daughter, and a third to chat with your boss. But these are three separate chats; your friend, your daughter, and your boss can't interact with each other. (Unless they open up separate chat windows to each other, of course.) You're talking to each one individually, not collectively.

Who's Chatting with Whom?

So who uses this chat thing, anyway?

Not surprisingly, Facebook chat is heavily used by younger members and less so by older ones. It's much the same as with text messages on your cell phone; kids do it more often than their parents.

This means, of course, that Facebook chat could be a great way to actually get some face time with your kids. You can't get them to talk at the dinner table (assuming they even come to dinner anymore), you can't get them to return email messages (they might not even use their email accounts), but you can probably get them to answer a chat request. They're online seemingly 24/7, always have Facebook open in their browsers, and are comfortable doing the chat thing. It's second nature to them, so you might as well take advantage of it.

Not that you want to overdo it, of course; you never want to push things too hard with your kids. But when you need to talk to your kids, you should see if they're online and, if so, ask them to chat with you. Now, an exchange of short text messages will never be confused with a heartfelt face-to-face conversation, but it's better than nothing. You'd be surprised how willing your children are to "talk" with you in this fashion; it's because you're meeting them on their own ground.

Chatting in Facebook

As you can see, Facebook's text chat is a great way to keep in touch with your online friends. You can even conduct multiple chat sessions at the same time—which the youngsters seem to be good at, but us oldsters might find a little daunting, multitasking-wise.

Seeing Who's Online

To chat with someone, both of you have to be online and signed into the Facebook site. How do you know, then, which of your friends are available to chat?

The first place to look is on your Facebook Home page. At the bottom of the left sidebar, as shown in Figure 10.1, is a box that says Friends on Chat. As you might suspect, this box lists those of your friends who are currently online and logged onto Facebook.

Figure 10.1. *The Friends on Chat box.*

Or at least some of them. Unfortunately, this isn't quite a complete list. I'm not even sure how Facebook puts this list together. Is it your most favorite friends? (And if so, how does Facebook know?) Is it the friends you communicate with most often? I don't know. But I do know this little box doesn't always show me everyone who's available to chat.

Instead, you want to display the more complete chat list that pops up from the bottom corner of every Facebook page. If you have enough friends and a wide enough web browser, the chat list displays in a Chat sidebar on the far right side of the Facebook page.

Figure 10.2 shows Facebook's Chat panel, which displays a full list of online friends, organized by the custom friends lists you create. (You learned about friends lists in Chapter 7, "Organizing Groups of Friends," if you recall.) Your custom lists appear first, with everybody not in a list appearing in the Other Friends section. So, for example, if you've created a custom list of family members labeled Family, online family members appear first in the Family section.

Figure 10.2. *The Chat panel, which displays all your online friends; those who are available to chat have a green circle next to their names.*

Within each separate list, your online friends are organized into two sections. At the top of each list are friends who have a full green circle by their names; these friends are online and active, which means they're available to chat. Beneath these names are those with a blue half-moon by their names. These friends are online but idle.

You can open a chat with anyone listed in the Chat pane, whether they're currently active or idle.

Starting a Chat Session

When you want to start chatting with someone, it's a relatively simple process. Here's how it works:

1. From the Chat panel, click the name of the person you want to chat with. This opens a new chat panel for this person, as shown in Figure 10.3.

Figure 10.3. *Chatting in real time with a Facebook friend.*

2. Type a text message in the bottom text box and press Enter.

Your messages, along with your friend's responses, appear in consecutive order within the chat panel. Continue typing new messages as you want.

It's pretty simple, really. You open a chat panel, you start typing, and that's that. When you're done chatting, you can close the chat window by clicking the X at the top of the panel.

By the way, you can display your chat in a larger window if you like. All you have to do is open the main Chat panel, click the Options button, and click Pop Out Chat. This opens a new Chat window, like the one shown in Figure 10.4.

Note

When another user invites you to chat, you hear a short sound and see a new chat panel for that person open on your Facebook page. Start typing to reply to your friend's initial message.

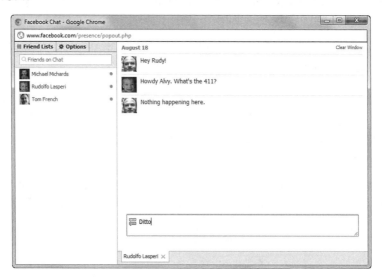

Figure 10.4. *Chatting in a larger Chat window.*

There's nothing really special about this, other than it's a bigger chat space than you have on the normal Facebook page. To close this Chat window and return to the normal Chat panel, click the Options button and select Pop Out Chat.

Managing Your Chat Settings

There are a handful of settings you can configure for your Facebook chat sessions. You get to them by clicking the Options button in the Chat panel.

Here's what you find, as shown in Figure 10.5:

- **Go Offline.** Click this if you don't want to chat while you're browsing the Facebook site. You're still logged on, but your friends don't know you're there. To return to online status, just click the Chat button at the bottom of the browser window.

- **Pop-Out Chat.** As described previously, this opens your chat panel into a larger chat window.

- **Play Sound for New Messages.** This one is checked "on" by default. Uncheck it to not play a sound when you get a new chat request.

- **Keep Online Friends Window Open.** Check this option to keep the Chat panel displayed, even when you return to the underlying Facebook page.

- **Show Only Names in Online Friends.** By default, Facebook displays a small thumbnail picture of each person who's online. Check this option to display names only with no photos.

Figure 10.5. *Configuring Facebook's chat options.*

In addition, you can select which of your custom friends lists to display in the Chat panel. Click the Friend Lists button and check those lists you want to display; uncheck those you don't want to see.

Getting Real Face Time with Video Chat

Text chat is fine, but chatting face-to-face is better. That's why Facebook recently launched a new video chat feature, so you can talk via webcam with your Facebook friends, right in your web browser; it's easy to use and quite useful.

Understanding Video Chat

Facebook has been working for the past year or so to revamp all its messaging-related features. It started with the new Messages feature, which consolidates all Facebook messages (private messages, emails, and such) in a single hub, as discussed in Chapter 9, "Exchanging Private Messages." The effort continued with the introduction of Facebook's video chat feature, which lets any two Facebook friends with webcams get a little face time with each other, in real time.

This new video chat feature is powered by Skype, the leader in Internet voice and video calling. It's part of an even larger merging of technologies between the two companies, which also manifests itself in increased Facebook connectivity within the Skype service.

Why is Facebook video chat important? It's a huge step forward in enabling person-to-person communication on the Facebook social network, without having to make all such communication public. More practically, it enables just about any Facebook user with a webcam to have a face-to-face conversation with any other Facebook user and no other software to run. The entire conversation takes place in your web browser on the Facebook site. There's virtually nothing to set up, and chatting with any Facebook friend is as easy as clicking a button.

Facebook video chat is also interesting in that it marks a relatively tight integration between Facebook and Skype. Not only does Skype power Facebook's video chat, the service also gets access to Facebook's News Feed, friends lists, and the like. It's almost like the two services have fused to some degree.

All that's fine and good, but why would you be interested in video chat? Personally, I find it quite useful to keep in touch with loved ones when we're apart. It's great to see what my grandkids are up to when they haven't visited for a while; they're big hams when chatting into their mom's webcam.

Video chat is also useful for conducting business meetings with people in far-away offices. It's faster than email, more personal than instant messaging, and cheaper than making a phone call. (Cheaper means it's free.) A few clicks of the mouse and you're having a productive meeting.

Launching a Video Chat

The first time you use Facebook's video chat, you are prompted to download and install the necessary background chat applet. Follow the onscreen instructions to do so. After everything is installed, it's quite easy to start a video chat. In fact, there are two ways to do so.

The first way is to go to a friend's profile page on the Facebook site. If this person has video chat set up, You see a new Call button at the top right of the profile page; click this button to start the call.

Figure 10.6. *Initiating a video chat from a friend's profile page.*

Another approach is to display the Chat list and click the name of the friend you want to chat with. When the Chat window appears, click the Start a Video Call button (camera icon) at the top of the window.

Figure 10.7. *Initiating a video chat from the chat window.*

However you get started, conducting a video call is equally simple. Your friend appears in a big window that sits on top of the Facebook page, as you can see in Figure 10.8; your picture is in a smaller window at the top left. All you have to do is talk.

Figure 10.8. *Conducting a Facebook video chat.*

When you're ready to close the chat, hover over the chat window, and then click the X at the top-right corner.

Integrating Facebook with Skype

The same week Facebook announced its Skype-powered video chat, Skype announced a handful of useful Facebook integration features into the latest Windows version of its client software. This might be useful if you're already a Skype user.

After you've upgraded to Skype for Windows version 5.5, you are prompted to connect your Facebook and Skype accounts. You need to do this to take advantage of all the new features.

When you're connected, you find that all your Facebook contacts are now Skype contacts. There's a new Facebook tab in the Contacts sidebar; click this tab to view a list of all your Facebook friends. (Your normal Skype contacts still appear on the Contacts tab next to the Facebook tab.)

Click a friend's name to view that person's contact info in the big pane on the right. From here you can initiate an audio (but surprisingly not a video) call by clicking the Call Phone button. You can also start a text chat with this person simply by typing some text into the text box at the bottom of the big pane. Your ongoing chat appears in the main section of this pane.

Close the pane for the current friend or contact to view Skype's normal set of tabs. Here you find another Facebook tab; click this tab to view the contents of your Facebook News Feed, arranged in multiple columns. You have the option of displaying all status updates or only those from your Skype contacts who are also Facebook friends.

You can also post new Facebook status updates from Skype's Facebook tab. Just enter your update into the box at the top of the page and press Enter. It's just like being on Facebook, expect you're still on Skype—which means you can effectively use Skype for almost all your online communications, including those with Facebook friends.

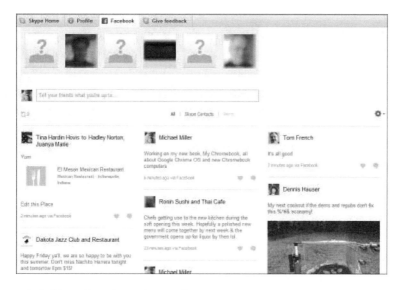

Figure 10.9. *Your Facebook News Feed on Skype.*

Chatting Versus Private Messages

When it comes to talking privately with someone on Facebook, which should you use: the chat feature or private messages?

It kind of comes down to who you're talking to and why. If it's someone you don't talk to that often or you have something long to say, use private messages. If it's someone you see all the time and just need to drop a short note—and they're online, of course—use chat.

The online thing is important. You can't chat with someone who isn't there. You can, however, send a message to someone who's not online at the time. They'll read your message the next time they log onto Facebook—which might not be today and might not be tomorrow.

You can be sure, however, of getting your message across to someone who's online now and willing to chat. That makes chat ideal for talking to and collaborating with colleagues during work hours.

Chat is also good for talking to younger friends and family members, like your own children. They're likely to be on Facebook all hours of the day and night, which makes them uniquely available to chat. And, because it's more difficult to ignore a chat request than it is a message dumped in their inbox, you're more likely to actually connect with them—which, knowing kids these days, is a big deal.

Chapter 11

Sharing Family Pictures

Here's something that I find somewhat amazing: Facebook is one of the largest photo-sharing sites on the Web. Nothing against Flickr or Shutterfly, but more and more people are using Facebook to share their photos with friends and family.

Why is this? It's because Facebook is such a big community, period. It's also because Facebook makes it so easy to upload and share photos. Bottom line: If you're on Facebook and your friends and family are also, then Facebook is as good a way as any to give everyone a peek at your pictures.

Understanding Photo Sharing on Facebook

Facebook is a social network, and one of the ways we connect socially is through pictures. We track our progress through life as a series of pictures, documenting events small and large, from picnics in the backyard to family vacations to births, graduations, and weddings and everything else that transpires.

People of our age have collected a lot of pictures over the years, dating back from our childhoods through our children's childhoods and possibly to their children's childhoods. In my household, we have literally tens of thousands of pictures, most in digital format now (either shot that way or scanned in), starting with my own baby pictures (and those of my wife, of course) and ending with pictures we shot yesterday of the grandkids. We're always taking new pictures and love to share them with other family members.

Sharing pictures is also a great way for old friends to catch up on what we've been doing in the intervening years. It's fun to see pictures of friends' kids and grandkids; it's not quite the same as being there, but it certainly helps.

Fortunately for all of us Facebook members, Facebook is a great site for sharing photos with friends and family. That's because it's fairly easy to share photos on Facebook. You can share a photo as part of status update or attach a photo to a private message. You can even create your own photo albums and share the contents with your Facebook friends.

Facebook Photo Sharing: The Old Way

In the past, photo sharing on Facebook was pretty much limited to viewing, not downloading. That's because Facebook didn't accept high-resolution photographs. Oh, you could choose a high-res (multi-megapixel) photo to upload, but Facebook would automatically convert it to a picture of no more than 640 pixels wide. It didn't matter if you had a 10 megapixel digital camera that produced 3600 x 2400 pixel photos; Facebook still converted them to 604 x 400 pixel pictures.

Now, a 604 x 400 photo is (arguably) okay for viewing in a web browser on a computer screen, but it's not good enough to print; the resolution is way too low to look good on photo paper. That might be why Facebook didn't have a "download photo" link or button. Facebook's low-res photos weren't good enough to print, so why bother downloading them?

This is why, in the previous edition of this book, I recommended *against* using Facebook as your primary photo-sharing site. I wrote that "Facebook is great for viewing other people's photos and for letting them look at yours. But if you want others to download or print your photos, or if you want to download or print other people's photos, Facebook leaves a lot to be desired. For this type of archival sharing, a site such as Shutterfly or Snapfish would be a better choice."

And that's the way it used to be.

Facebook Photo Sharing: The New Way

Well, Facebook heard my complaints. (Actually, they probably didn't hear my individual complaints at all, but rather the complaints of millions of other users.) Late in 2010, Facebook rolled out a new Photo Uploader and introduced new photo-sharing features—all of which combine to make Facebook a much better site for viewing and downloading high-quality digital photos.

What did Facebook change? Here are the highlights:

- **Higher resolution photos.** Instead of limiting your photos to 604 pixels wide, Facebook now lets users upload photos up to 2048 pixels wide—up to eight times bigger than before. That means you can share pictures with enough resolution to create great-looking photo prints. It's a huge improvement, one that makes Facebook ideal not just for viewing photos but also for downloading and printing them.

- **New Photo Uploader.** Facebook now offers a new Photo Uploader, not to be confused with the old New Photo Uploader. (Yeah, they could have done something more intuitive with the name thing.) The new Photo Uploader uses Flash technology to help you more easily choose photos to upload and then adds information for each photo. It works better than the old uploader and is easier to use, as well.

- **New photo viewer.** Not only do you get an improved environment for uploading photos, the experience of viewing photos is also better. The new photo viewer displays the chosen photo in a lightbox in the middle of the current screen without opening a new page. There's also a much-needed Download link, which makes it a lot easier to download and ultimately print the photos you like.

Bottom line: Facebook is finally a great site for both viewing and downloading digital photos. You can share all your family photos and be assured that friends and family can download and print the ones they like best.

How Facebook Photo Sharing Works

As to the nitty gritty of how Facebook's photo sharing works, it's actually quite intuitive. The photos you upload are accessible from your Profile page, organized into individual photo albums, just like you do (or used to do) with physical photo albums. Some users have hundreds and thousands of photos available for viewing on the Facebook site.

Uploading photos takes little more than a few clicks of the mouse; it's easy enough that anyone can do it. Your photos are automatically visible to everyone on the Facebook site, so your friends and potential friends can view them.

Note

Facebook says you're only supposed to upload photos for which you have permission. That means uploading your own photos, not photos you've ripped off from someone or someplace else.

Facebook also lets you *tag* people in your photos. This lets you identify who is in each photo. So, for example, if you have a photo of you and your cousin Velma, you can tag both yourself and Velma in the photo. This photo appears in your own photo albums, of course, but it also shows up on Velma's Photos page, in the Photos and Videos of Velma section.

Uploading Photos to Facebook

When it comes to sharing photos on Facebook, it all starts with the Photo Uploader. This is where you choose your photos to upload and add information for each photo.

Uploading to a New Photo Album

I start by assuming that this is the first time you've uploaded photos to Facebook and thus need to create a new photo album to host these photos. Follow these steps:

1. Click your name on the Facebook toolbar to go to your Profile page.

2. From your Profile page, click the Photos graphics near the top of the page.

3. When the Photos page appears, as shown in Figure 11.1, click the Add Photos button.

Figure 11.1. *Getting ready to upload photos.*

4. When the Upload Photos dialog box appears, as shown in Figure 11.2, click the Select Photos button.

Figure 11.2. *Getting ready to select photos to upload.*

5. When the Select File(s) to Upload or Open window appears, select the photos you want to upload; hold down the Ctrl key to select multiple photos. Click Open when done.

6. A new Upload Photos dialog box, shown in Figure 11.3, appears while your photos are being uploaded. Enter the name of the new photo album into the Name of Album box.

The file upload window you see depends on which web browser you're using. If you're using Internet Explorer, you see the Select File(s) to Upload window. If you're using Google Chrome, you see the Open window. It's a browser thing.

Figure 11.3. *Entering information about your new photo album.*

7. Enter the (optional) location where the photos were shot into the Location box.

8. Enter the quality you want these pictures to be viewed in. Select Standard to create a somewhat low-resolution version or High Resolution if you want to retain the quality of the original photo.

Tip

Select High Resolution if you want your friends to download print-quality photos—but know that it takes longer for you to upload High Resolution pictures.

9. Click the Share Album With button to select whom you want to share the album with— Public, Friends, or Custom. You can also opt to share with members of specific friends lists.

10. Click the Create Album button.

11. If there are people in photos you've uploaded, you see the Who's in These Photos? page. See the "Tagging a Friend's Face" section, later in this chapter, for further instructions, and then click the Save Tags button.

12. If there are no people in the photos you uploaded, you see the Edit Album page, as shown in Figure 11.4. From here you can add descriptions for each photo; select the Edit Photos tab and enter descriptive text into the Description box. Click the Publish Now button when done.

Figure 11.4. *Editing information about your photo album.*

You now see the page for this photo album. A status update announcing the photo uploads is also posted automatically, so your chosen friends are alerted to your new photos.

Uploading to an Existing Photo Album

After you've created a photo album, you can upload additional photos to that album. Here's how:

1. From your Profile page, click Photos in the sidebar.

2. When the Photos page appears, click the photo album you want to upload to.

3. When the album page appears, click the Add Photos button.

4. When the Upload Photos dialog box appears, click the Select Photos button.

5. When the Select File(s) to Upload or Open window appears, select the photos you want to upload; hold down the Ctrl key to select multiple photos. Click Open when done.

6. When the new Upload Photos dialog box appears, as shown in Figure 11.5, select either Standard or High Resolution.

Figure 11.5. *Uploading a photo to an existing album.*

7. When your photos are done uploading, click the Done button.

8. If you see the Who's in These Photos? page, feel free to tag friends in the photos. Click Save Tags when done.

9. If, instead, you see the Edit Album page, enter descriptions for the photos you just uploaded, tag any friends in the photos, and select a new album cover if you like. Click the Publish Now button when done.

Tagging Friends in Your Photos

In the previous section I touched on the subject of tagging—the act of identifying specific people in your photographs. As you've just seen, when you upload a photo to Facebook, you're prompted to tag each person who appears in the photo; you can also go back and tag people in your photos at any time.

When you tag a Facebook friend in a photo, a status update announcing that tag is placed in the friend's News Feed, and the photo now appears among the friend's Facebook photos. This makes it easy for your friends to view themselves and other friends in your photos.

Understanding Facebook's Face Recognition Feature

Until recently this tagging process has been completely manual. However, Facebook has added face recognition technology that attempts to automatically figure out which friends are in your pictures. The goal is to make tagging pictures easier so that more people do it.

Let's face it; if you upload a ton of pictures, tagging each photo manually can be somewhat tedious. Imagine uploading a hundred or so family reunion photos, and having to tag each and every appearance of Uncle Ralph by hand—all two dozen of them.

Facebook attempts to make this process easier by employing basic face detection technology, the same kind used in today's digital cameras, to identify where the faces are in the photos you upload. This works whenever you upload a photo with people in it; Facebook identifies that there are faces in the picture and puts a little box around each face.

Next, Facebook attempts to group similar faces. That is, it tries to find multiple pictures of the same person, and then groups them together on the photo tagging page. You can then enter a single tag and have it applied to multiple photos. That's a one-tag approach to all two dozen of those photos of your Uncle Ralph.

Finally, Facebook's face recognition technology suggests tags for the faces it recognizes. Or at least, it tries to; to be honest, this technology isn't perfect and doesn't always identify the right people. It works best when you upload a photo of someone you've tagged previously and perhaps even multiple times in the past. (It kind of learns by example.) If the suggestion is correct, you can accept the tag. If not, just tag the person as you would normally.

Tagging a Friend's Face

To use Facebook's automatic face tagging feature, follow these steps:

1. Upload one or more digital photos with people in them, as previously described.

2. After the pictures are uploaded, Facebook displays the Who's in These Photos? page, shown in Figure 11.6. Each face in each picture is identified with a box around it; also notice that Facebook tries to group photos of the same person, if it can. If Facebook recognizes a person in a photo or groups of photos, it suggests a tag for that person. Click the suggested tag to accept it or click the X to reject it.

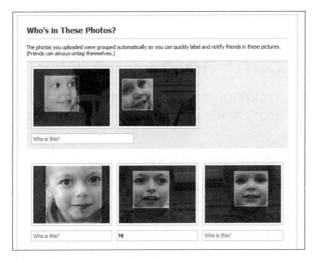

Figure 11.6. *Facebook identifies faces in photos and groups similar faces together.*

3. To manually tag any photo or group of photos, start entering that person's name in the Who Is This? box under the photo(s). Facebook displays a list of matching friends, as shown in Figure 11.7; click the appropriate name to tag the photo.

Figure 11.7. *Tagging faces in photos.*

4. When you're done tagging recently uploaded photos, scroll to the bottom of the Tag Your Friends page, and click the Save Tags button.

Your photos are now tagged, and your tagged friends are notified that they've been tagged.

Managing Your Photos and Albums

After you upload a lot of photos to Facebook, you might want to spend a little time editing your photos and organizing your albums.

Editing a Photo's Description

After a photo is uploaded, you can edit the description of that photo. Follow these steps:

1. Navigate to your Profile page, and select the Photos tab.

2. Click the album that contains the photo you want to edit.

3. When the album opens, click the photo you want to edit. This displays the photo page, like the one shown in Figure 11.8. Click the Edit link beneath the picture.

4. This opens the description panel, shown in Figure 11.9. Enter your description of the photo into the Add a Description box, or edit an existing description.

Figure 11.8. *A Facebook photo page.*

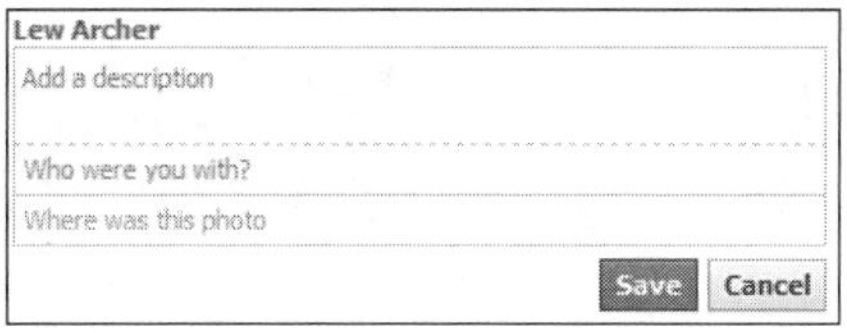

Lew Archer
Add a description

Who were you with?
Where was this photo

Save Cancel

Figure 11.9. *Editing a photo's description.*

5. If you were with other people when the photo was taken, enter their names into the Who Were You With? box.

6. To add locator information to the photo, enter where the photo was taken into the Where Was this Photo box.

7. Click the Save button.

Tagging Friends

As noted previously, you can tag friends in your photos at any point in time. Follow these steps:

1. Navigate to your Profile page, and click the Photos graphic.

2. Click the album that contains the photo you want to edit.

3. When the photo album opens, click the photo you want to edit.

4. When the photo page appears, click the Tag Photo button on the bottom right of the photo.

5. In the photo, click on the face of the person you want to tag.

6. Facebook now displays a box around the selected person, along with a list of suggested friends, as shown in Figure 11.10.

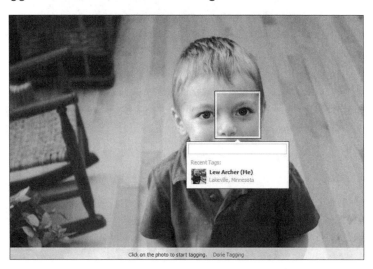

Figure 11.10. *Tagging a person in a photo.*

7. Click the correct friend's name in the list or enter the person's name into the text box. (You can also tag yourself in the photo, of course.)

8. Click the Done Tagging link.

By the way, it's also easy to remove a tag from a photo. Just navigate to the photo page, and you see the people tagged next to your name underneath the photo. (As in "Your Name with Someone Else," the someone else being the person tagged.) Hover over the name to untag and click Remove Tag.

Note

If you enter the name of a person who isn't a Facebook member, Facebook prompts you to enter that person's email address. Facebook then emails that person a link to the photo and invites him to join Facebook and become your friend.

Deleting a Photo

Deleting a photo from an album is also simple. Follow these steps:

1. Navigate to your Profile page, and click the Photos graphic.

2. Click the album that contains the photo you want to delete.

3. When the album opens, click the photo you want to delete.

4. When the photo page appears, click the Delete This Photo link.

Pretty simple, when all is said and done.

Adding a Description to a Photo Album

You can also add a description to a photo album. Follow these steps:

1. Navigate to your Profile page, and select the Photos tab.

2. Click the album you want to edit.

3. When the album opens, click the Add a Description link under the photos in the album.

4. This opens a text box. Enter your descriptive text into this box.

5. Click the Save button.

Deleting a Photo Album

To delete an entire photo album, including all the photos within, follow these steps:

1. Navigate to your Profile page, and click the Photos graphic.

2. Click the album you want to edit.

3. When the album page appears, click the Edit Album link at the top of the page.

4. When the Edit Album dialog box appears, click the Delete Album link.

5. When the confirmation dialog box appears, click the Delete Album button.

Sharing Photos with Others

Facebook makes it easy to share any photo you upload with others. You can share a photo publicly as a status update or privately via a message. Here's how it works:

1. Navigate to your Profile page, and click the Photos graphic.

2. Click the album that contains the photo you want to share.

3. When the album opens, click the photo you want to share.

4. When the photo page opens, click the Share link beneath the photo. This opens the Share This Photo window, as shown in Figure 11.11.

Figure 11.11. *Sharing a photo as a status update.*

5. To share this photo publicly via a status update, type a message to accompany the photo into the main text box, and then click the Share button.

6. To share this photo privately via private message, pull down the On Your Own Timeline list, and click In a Private Message. When the dialog box changes, as shown in Figure 11.12, enter the recipient's name into the Enter a Friend's Name box, enter an accompanying message into the Write Something box, and click the Share Photo button.

Share this Photo

Share: **In a private Message** ▼

Enter a friend's name

Write Something...

From the album: October 1, 2011
By Lew Archer

Share Photo | Cancel

Figure 11.12. *Sharing a photo via private message.*

Viewing Other People's Photos

Sharing your own photos is only part of the fun. You can also spend a lot of time viewing the photos that your friends have uploaded to Facebook.

Viewing Photos and Photo Albums

To view a friend's photos, go to her Profile page, and click the Photos graphic in the information section. As you can see in Figure 11.13, the top part of this page displays your friend's photo albums; the bottom part of the page displays photos where your friend is tagged. Click the See All link to view additional albums and photos.

Figure 11.13. *Viewing a friend's photos.*

To view the pictures in an album, click that album's name or thumbnail. This displays a page full of pictures, as shown in Figure 11.14. To return to your friend's Photos tab, click the Albums link at the top of the page.

To view a given picture, click that photos' thumbnail. The photo viewer pops up on top of the page, as shown in Figure 11.14. You move to the next photo in the album by click-

Note

The Profile Pictures album is automatically generated by Facebook and contains all the photos used as Profile pictures.

ing the right arrow; there's no need to close the photo, and then reopen the next one. Keep clicking the right arrow to move through all the photos in the album; click the left arrow to go back through the previously viewed photos. To close the viewer and get back to the photo album, just click the X (close) button at the top right of the viewer.

Figure 11.14. *Viewing photos in a photo album.*

Figure 11.15. *Viewing a photo.*

Adding Your Comments

You can easily comment on any picture you view to let your friend know what you think about it. There's a Write a Comment box under the photo; type your comment into the box, and then press Enter.

You can also just "like" a photo. Click the Like link to voice your approval.

Tagging Yourself in a Photo

If you find yourself in a friend's photo, you can tag yourself therein. (You can also tag other people, not just yourself.) You do this the same way you add tags to your own photo. Click the Tag Photo button at the bottom right corner of the photo, click your face in the photo, and then check your name in the accompanying list. Click Done Tagging to make it stick.

Sharing a Photo

See a friend's photo that you'd like to share with others? You can share friends' photos just as you can share your own. Click the Share link under the photo, and then opt to share as a public status update on your own timeline or via private message. Enter an accompanying message, and then click the Share Photo button.

Downloading a Photo

To download a copy of this photo, click the Download link underneath the photo. This saves the photo to your hard drive. You can then print the photo yourself or send it to a photo-printing service to make prints.

Printing a Photo

Now we come to something a little more difficult. What do you do if you want to print a friend's photo? There's no "print" button on the page, after all.

What you have to do is take advantage of your web browser's capability to print photos on a web page. If you're using Internet Explorer, for example, all you have to do is right-click the photo and select Print Picture from the pop-up menu. Other browsers have similar commands. Follow the onscreen instructions from here to print this photo to your selected printer.

Note

If a photo were uploaded in high resolution, you download a high-resolution copy. If the photo was uploaded in just standard resolution, you get a lower-resolution copy—probably not suitable for printing.

Face Tagging: Too Much of a Good Thing?

At first glance, Facebook's face recognition feature seems like a good thing; it should reduce the amount of time you spend tagging your photos. That said, do you really want Facebook automatically identifying you in any picture your friends upload? Some view this as a potential invasion of privacy and not a good thing at all.

First, realize that some folks simply don't want to be tagged in photos uploaded by others. This is understandable because you don't have any control over the photograph. Imagine a photo of you passed out on the floor after a wild party; you probably don't want this circulating to coworkers and family. Now, if you took the photo, you can simply not upload it. But if a friend took and uploaded the photo, and then tagged you in it, you're put in an embarrassing situation over which you have little control. Better not to be tagged by others, at least in this sort of situation.

It gets worse the easier Facebook makes it to add tags; it's especially onerous when Facebook actually does the suggesting. With automatic face recognition, you're more likely to be identified in photos you'd rather not be posted.

Then there's the issue of whether you really want Facebook (or any other site, for that matter) to know what you look like. Many users are uncomfortable with the chance that Facebook might use your face without your permission.

Fortunately, Facebook lets you opt out of being tagged in friends' photos—including those pictures where your face is automatically recognized. Just go to Facebook's Privacy Settings page, scroll to the How Tags Work section, and click the Edit Settings link. When the How Tags Work dialog box appears, click the Timeline Review item and, in the resulting dialog box, click the Turn on the Timeline Review button. This lets you manually approve or disapprove all posts (including pictures) in which friends have tagged you.

You can also exclude yourself from Facebook's automatic face recognition feature—that is, not have Facebook recommend your name when it recognizes your face in someone else's photo. Go back to the How Tags Work dialog box, click the Tag Suggestions item, and, in the resulting dialog box, click the button from Enabled to Disabled. This will help, just a little, in protecting your privacy online.

Chapter 12

Sharing Home Movies

Now you know how to share your digital photos with friends and family on Facebook. But did you know you can also use Facebook to share your home movies? All you have to do is have your movies in digital format (which you probably do, if you're shooting with a relatively new camcorder). You can then upload your digital video files for all your Facebook friends to see.

And that's not all; if you have videos already uploaded to YouTube, you can share those videos in your Facebook status updates. In fact, you can share just about *any* YouTube video—even those from other users—with your Facebook friends. It's pretty cool, after you get started.

The Ins and Outs of Sharing Videos on Facebook

Facebook lets you upload just about any type of video and share it as a status update—which means all your friends should see it as part of their News Feeds. Your uploaded videos also end up on a Video tab on your Profile page, much the same way that uploaded photos end up on your Photos tab.

Shooting Videos for Facebook

Where do you get videos to upload? It all starts with a digital video camera, or what some people call a camcorder. Today's camcorders save your movies in one of these common video file formats, which you can then transfer to your personal computer for editing.

Any video camera does the job; it doesn't have to be a fancy one. In fact, those inexpensive little "flip" cameras are just fine for Facebook use. But in practice, you can use any video camera you happen to own.

It helps, of course, if your camera is a digital one (all new ones are), as a digital camcorder by nature saves your movies as digital video files, which is what you upload to Facebook. Even if you have an older camcorder that stores videos on old-school videotapes, there are ways to transfer your movies from tape to computer files.

What to Upload

What kinds of videos can you upload to Facebook? Home movies are common, although you can upload other types of videos, as long as you're not uploading any copyrighted material. That means you can't upload commercial videos or videos that contain commercial music in the background.

You can upload videos already stored as digital files or create new videos in real-time from your computer's webcam. Videos must be no more than 20 minutes long and no more than 1024MB in size. Facebook accepts videos in the following file formats:

• 3G2	• M2TS	• MTS
• 3GP	• M4V	• NSV
• 3GPP	• MKV	• OGM
• ASF	• MOD	• OGV
• AVI	• MOV	• QT
• DAT	• MP4	• TOD
• DIVX	• MPE	• TS
• DV	• MPEG	• VOB
• F4V	• MPEG4	• WMV
• FLV	• MPG	

That's pretty much any video file format that's in use today.

As to resolution, aspect ratio, and all that other technical stuff you probably don't know much about, not to worry; Facebook accepts videos at any resolution in either standard or widescreen aspect ratio. So if you have a video camera that shoots in high-definition widescreen, Facebook plays back your videos in all their HD glory. And if your camcorder is an older one without HD capabilities, that's okay, too.

Editing Your Videos

I do recommend editing your movies, as opposed to uploading raw video files. Editing lets you get rid of those scenes that don't work, for whatever reason (bad lighting, jittery camerawork, awkward action) and creates a more concise movie. Today's video-editing programs let you cut and rearrange scenes, insert transitions between scenes, and add title cards, graphics, and other special effects. The end result can look quite professional, with little effort on your part.

Fortunately, some of the most versatile and easiest-to-use video-editing programs are free or relatively low cost. The free programs are those that come with your computer's operating system: Windows Movie Maker (for Windows users) and iMovie (if you have an Apple Mac). If you need more features than these programs offer, check out one of these programs:

- Adobe Premiere Elements (www.adobe.com/products/premiereel/, $99.99)
- Pinnacle Studio HD (www.pinnaclesys.com, $59.99)
- Sony Vegas Movie Studio HD (www.sonycreativesoftware.com/moviestudiohd/, $44.95)

Uploading Your Videos

To share a home movie on Facebook, all you have to do is click a few buttons. Here's how it works:

1. Navigate to your Profile page, and select the Photos graphic in the information section at the top of the page.

2. When the Photos page displays, as shown in Figure 12.1, click the Add Videos button in the top-right corner.

Figure 12.1. *Getting ready to upload a video from your Photos page.*

3. When the Create a New Video page appears, as shown in Figure 12.2, make sure the File Upload tab is selected, and then click the Choose File or Browse button.

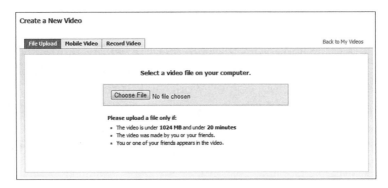

Figure 12.2. *Uploading a video file.*

4. When the Open or Choose File to Upload dialog box appears, navigate to and select the file to upload, and then click the Open button.

5. While the video is uploading, Facebook displays the page shown in Figure 12.3. Enter a title for this video in the Title box.

Figure 12.3. *Entering information for an uploaded video.*

6. Enter a short description of this video in the Description box.

7. To tag people who appear in the video, enter their names into the In This Video box.

8. Click the Privacy button to determine who can watch this video: Public, Friends of Friends, Friends, or Customize.

9. Click the Save Info button.

When the file is finished uploading (which can take a bit of time, especially if you have a long video or are on a slow Internet connection), it appears on your Photos page.

Recording a Webcam Video

You can also upload videos recorded from your computer's webcam in real time. This is a great way to do a quick–and-dirty video for your Facebook friends, no fancy hardware or software required (beyond the webcam, of course).

Here's how to do it:

1. Navigate to your Profile page and select Photos.

2. From the Photos page, click the Add Videos button.

3. When the Create a New Video page appears, select the Record Video tab.

4. You now see a live shot from your computer's webcam, as shown in Figure 12.4. Click the red Record button to begin recording.

5. When you're done recording, click the Stop button.

6. You can now watch the video you just recorded, as shown in Figure 12.5, by clicking the Play button.

Note

If you're prompted to okay the use of the Flash plug-in for recording, check Agree.

Figure 12.4. *Getting ready to record a webcam video.*

Figure 12.5. *Saving your webcam video.*

7. If you don't like what you see, click the Reset button to start over.

8. To save the video you just recorded, click the Save button.

9. Facebook now displays the Edit Video page, as shown in Figure 12.6. Enter the names of you or any of your Facebook friends appearing in this video into the In This Video box.

10. Enter a title for this video into the Title box.

11. Enter a short description of this video into the Description box.

Figure 12.6. *Editing information for a webcam video.*

12. Click the Privacy button to determine who can watch this video.

13. If multiple thumbnails are available, go to the Choose a Thumbnail section and select which thumbnail image you want displayed for this video.

14. Click the Save button.

Editing Video Information

If you have been following my instructions, you've already entered information about your videos, as well as tagged any of your friends appearing in a video. If you didn't enter this info, however, you can enter it at any later time—or edit information you'd like to change.

Here's how to edit your video information:

1. Navigate to your Profile page, and click the Photos graphic.

2. When the Photos page appears, go to the Your Photos section, and click the Videos link.

3. When the Your Videos page appears, as shown in Figure 12.7, click the video you want to edit.

4. When the video page appears, click the Edit This Video link, beneath the video.

5. You now see the Edit Video page, as shown in Figure 12.8. Enter or change any of the following information: Title, Description, Privacy level, or Thumbnail image.

Figure 12.7. *All the videos on your Your Videos page.*

Figure 12.8. *Use this page to edit information about your video.*

6. To remove a tag for someone appearing in the video, click the X next to that person's name.

7. To add a new tag, enter that person's name into the In This Video box.

8. Save your changes by clicking the Save button.

Sharing Uploaded Videos

Just as with photos, any video you've uploaded to Facebook can be shared publicly or privately with your friends and family—which is a great way for the people you love to see your home movies. Here's how to do it:

1. Navigate to your Profile page, and click the Photos graphic.

2. When the Photos page appears, go to the Your Photos section, and click the Videos link.

3. When the Your Videos page appears, click the thumbnail image of the video you want to share.

4. When the page for the selected video opens, click the Share button to display the Share This Video window, as shown in Figure 12.9.

Share this Video

📃 Share: **On your own timeline** ▼   👥 Friends ▼

Playing in the Sprinkler [HD]
By Michael Miller

5:46 Added about 2 months ago

Share Video   Cancel

Figure 12.9. *Posting a video as a status update.*

5. To share this video publicly as a status update, enter an accompanying message in the Write Something box, and then click the Share Video button.

6. To share this video privately via Facebook Messages, click the On Your Own Timeline button, and click In a Private Message. When the window changes, enter the recipient's name into the Enter a Friend's Name box, enter an accompanying message into the Write Something box, and click the Share Video button.

> **✔ Tip**
>
> You can also embed any Facebook video into your own web page or blog. To get the embed code, go to the video's page, and click the Embed This Video link. When the Embed Your Video dialog box appears, copy the embed code, and paste it into your web page's underlying HTML code.

Posting YouTube Videos

Here's another way to share videos on Facebook. If you're familiar with the YouTube video sharing site, you can post any YouTube video as a Facebook status update.

That's right; you can share *any* YouTube video on Facebook. This includes videos you've uploaded to the YouTube site, as well as any other public YouTube video uploaded by any other user, including all those videos of cute kittens and laughing babies. It's a great way to share not only your own videos but also any videos you find funny, useful, or whatever.

There are two keys to posting a YouTube video file to Facebook. First, you have to have a YouTube account. (Don't worry; it's free.) Second, you need to link your YouTube and Facebook accounts, which is pretty much a one-click operation.

From there, it's all a matter of finding a YouTube video you want to share, and then clicking the appropriate buttons. Here's how it works:

1. Go to YouTube (www.youtube.com) and log in to your YouTube account.

2. Navigate to the video you want to post to Facebook.

3. Underneath the video player, click the Share button to expand the Share panel, as shown in Figure 12.10.

Note

YouTube is the world's largest online video community with hundreds of millions of videos available for viewing. Learn more about YouTube in my companion book, *Sams Teach Yourself YouTube in 10 Minutes* (Michael Miller, Sams Publishing, 2009).

Tip

Because YouTube video files can be twice as large (2GB) as those allowed for direct uploading to Facebook, embedding a YouTube video might be a better way to share larger video files, such as those recorded in high definition.

Figure 12.10. *Getting ready to share a YouTube video.*

4. Click the Facebook button.

5. The first time you share a YouTube video, you see the Facebook Login window. Enter your email address and Facebook password, and then click the Login button. (You won't see this window again.)

6. When the Share This Link window appears, as shown in Figure 12.11, enter an accompanying message into the Write Something box.

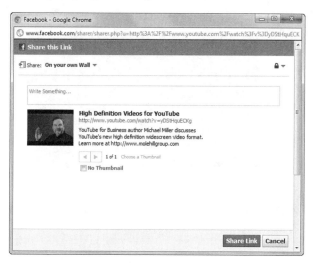

Figure 12.11. *Sharing a YouTube video.*

7. Select a thumbnail to display (if more than one thumbnail image is available) or check the No Thumbnail option to post the video without a corresponding thumbnail image.

8. Click the Share Link button.

This video is now posted as a status update to Facebook, like the one shown in Figure 12.12. To play a YouTube video embedded as a status update, simply click the video name or thumbnail in the post. A larger video player displays within the Facebook News Feed, complete with playback controls, as shown in Figure 12.13. Alternatively, click the title of the video in the News Feed and you open that video's playback page on the YouTube site.

Figure 12.12. *A YouTube video shared via Facebook status update.*

Figure 12.13. *Watching a YouTube video on Facebook.*

Watching Your Friends' Videos

With all this talk about sharing your own videos, how do you watch videos that your friends have posted to Facebook? There are two ways to go about it.

Watching a Video in the News Feed

When a friend first uploads a video, it should show up in your News Feed, like the one shown in Figure 12.14. Click the video; it now gets larger on the page and starts to play, as shown in Figure 12.15. To control the video, simply hover your cursor over it; the various playback controls display, from left to right:

- Pause/Play

- Time slider (slide to move to another point in the video)

- Elapsed time/Total time

- Mute/Volume

- Full screen

Figure 12.14. *A video posted as a Facebook status update.*

Figure 12.15. *Watching a Facebook video, complete with playback controls.*

To pause playback, click the Pause button, which then changes to a Play button. To resume playback, click the Play button.

To move to another point in the video, click and drag the Time Slider left (earlier) or right (later). To mute the sound, click the Mute button; click this button again to unmute the sound. To adjust the video's volume, click and drag across the Volume control. And to view the video full-screen, click the Full-Screen button; press Esc to exit full-screen mode.

Watching a Video on Its Own Page

You can also view any Facebook video on its own video page, actually a lightbox overlay on the current page, as shown in Figure 12.16. This page displays the video a bit larger than on the News Feed page, which is a good thing. On this page, click the video to begin playback, and then hover over the video to display the playback controls.

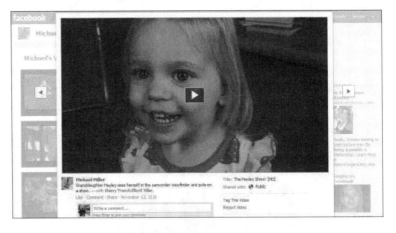

Figure 12.16. *A Facebook video playback page.*

The dedicated video page also displays more information about the video, including those people tagged in the video and any comments left by other viewers. To leave your comments, start typing into the Write a Comment box under the video, press Return when done.

Of course, you can also use this page to share this video with your other friends. Click the Share link to display the Share This Video dialog box, as shown in Figure 12.17. Enter your comments into the Write Something box, and then click the Share Video button to post this update as a status update of your own. If you prefer to share the video privately, click On Your Own Timeline button, and select In a Private Message; enter the recipient's name and your message, and then click the Share Video button.

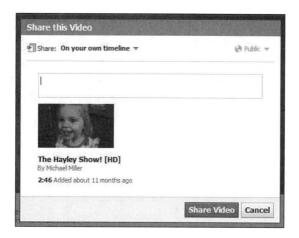

Figure 12.17. *Sharing a Facebook video.*

Video Resolution

When we're talking about videos, higher resolution is always better. In terms of video playback, a higher-resolution video looks sharper than one recorded at a lower resolution; there's just more detail in the picture. The best picture quality comes from so-called high-definition videos, which have the highest possible resolution.

Facebook lets you upload videos at any resolution, low to high, and you can watch videos recorded at any resolution, too. Great, you might think; I want to watch all my videos in the highest possible resolution.

The problem with this is that higher resolution means larger file sizes (more information in the video file), which then translates into longer download times. If you have a particularly slow Internet connection, this could result in stuttering playback or unwanted pauses while the download catches up to your viewing.

The solution, if you have a slow Internet connection, is to watch your videos at a lower resolution. You can do this when watching videos on their own playback pages on Facebook.

Facebook labels videos recorded at a higher-than-normal resolution as HQ videos. Videos recorded in high definition are labeled as HD videos. By default, Facebook's video playback page plays videos at their highest resolution. To play back a video at a lower resolution, click the View in Regular Quality link beneath the video. That should speed things up for you.

Chapter 13

Sharing Birthdays and Events

Being as Facebook is a social network, what could be more social than sharing important events with your friends? You can use Facebook to let your friends know of upcoming birthdays in your tribe, community gatherings, business meetings, parties, or you name it. It's all done via Facebook's Events feature, which lets you respond to other people's events and create events of your own.

Why You Might Like Events

To be honest, events are probably one of the least used features on Facebook. I'm not sure why; they're quite useful for scheduling get-togethers with friends, family members, and coworkers.

I guess it helps to understand exactly what an *event* is. On Facebook, an event is like an item on your personal schedule. Events can be small and private, like a doctor's appointment or dinner with a friend. Events can also be large and public, like a museum opening or family reunion.

As such, you can use events to invite friends to cocktail parties, soccer games, or community meetings. You can also use Facebook events to remember friends' birthdays.

The events you work with don't have to be real-world, physical events, either. You can schedule virtual events, such as inviting all your friends to watch a specific TV show on a given evening. You can also schedule online events, such as seminars and conferences on sites that offer such options. In other words, you don't have to meet someone in person to share an event with them.

There are tons of events scheduled on Facebook by other members of the site. The best way to find new events is by using the search box on the Facebook toolbar; you can also browse scheduled events being attended by your Facebook friends. When you find an event you want to attend, or when you've been invited to an event by a friend, you can then RSVP your intentions.

Of course, you can also create your own events. Maybe your child has a sporting event or concert coming up you want to invite family members to. Maybe you're hosting a big party for your real-world friends. Or maybe you just want to let everyone know about an important community gathering. Whatever the case, Facebook makes it relatively easy to create new events and invite some or all of your Facebook friends to these events.

Searching for and Attending Events

Let's start with the quest for new events to attend. You can search events by name, date, or type. Here's how it works:

1. Enter one or more keywords that describe the event into the Search box in the Facebook toolbar, and then click the Search (the magnifying glass) button or press Enter.

2. The search results page now displays, but these results include much more than just events. To display only events that match your query, click Events in the sidebar.

3. Facebook now displays those events that match your query, as shown in Figure 13.1. If you think you want to attend the event, click the RSVP button.

Note

Most event types have their own subtypes; the Subtypes list appears after you select a main event type. For example, if you select Causes, you can then drill down further by selecting Fundraiser, Protest, or Rally as a subtype.

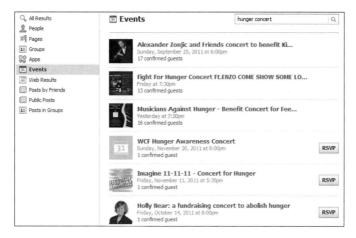

Figure 13.1. *Displaying events that match your search query.*

4. The RSVP to This Event dialog box displays, as shown in Figure 13.2. Check your intention (Attending, Maybe Attending, or Not Attending), add an optional note to the event's organizer, and then click the RSVP button.

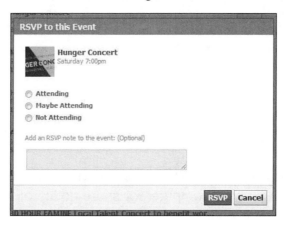

Figure 13.2. *RSVP'ing to an event.*

5. If you want to learn more about an event before RSVP'ing, click the event's title to view the Facebook page for that event.

RSVP'ing to Events

As you just saw, you can RSVP to an event directly from a search results page. You can also RSVP to an event from the Facebook page for that event, from a friend's status update post about an event, or from an email that a friend might send you about an event.

RSVP'ing from the Event Page

Let's start by going to the Facebook page for an event, seeing what's there, and then RSVP'ing or sharing notice of that event.

When you click on the title of an event anywhere on the Facebook site, you display the page for that event. As you can see in Figure 13.3, a typical Event page contains more information about the event itself—the start and end times, location, description, and even a list of guests attending.

Figure 13.3. *Viewing an event's Facebook page.*

You can use this page to RSVP to an event, download that event to any calendar application on your computer, or share notice of that event with your friends. Here's how it works:

1. To RSVP to an event, check the appropriate button: I'm Attending, Maybe, or No.

2. To download this event to your computer's calendar program, such as Microsoft Outlook, scroll to the bottom of the Event page, and click the Export Event link. This displays the Export Event dialog box, as shown in Figure 13.4. Check the Download Calendar Appointment option, and then click the Okay button.

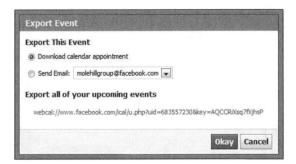

Figure 13.4. *Downloading event info to a calendar application.*

3. To email yourself a notice of this event, click the Export button on the Event page to display the Export Event dialog box, check the Send Email option, verify your email address, and then click the Okay button.

4. Likewise, you can also share notice of an event with your Facebook friends. To share an event as a public status update, click the Share link at the top of the Event page. This displays the Share This Event dialog box, as shown in Figure 13.5; enter some accompanying text, and then click the Share Event button.

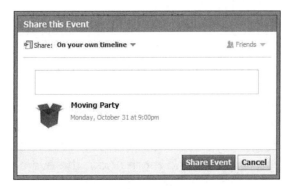

Figure 13.5. *Sharing an event as a status update.*

5. To email notice of an event to a friend via Facebook private message, click the Share button on the Event page to display the Share This Event dialog box. Click the On Your Own Timeline button, and select In a Private Message. When the dialog box changes, as shown in Figure 13.6, enter your friend's name into the Enter a Friend's Name box, enter a short message into the Write Something box, and then click the Share Event button.

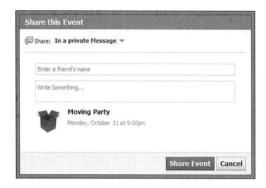

Figure 13.6. *Sharing an event via private message.*

RSVP'ing from a Status Update

Your friends sometimes post notice of upcoming events that they've created or are interested in. (Figure 13.7 shows how such an event looks in your News Feed.)

Figure 13.7. *An event notification in the Facebook News Feed.*

To respond directly to one of these status update notices, click the RSVP to This Event link. This displays the RSVP to This Event dialog box, where you can check Attending, Maybe Attending, or Not Attending, and then click the RSVP button. If you'd rather read more about the event in question, simply click the event's titles in the News Feed.

RSVP'ing from an Email Invitation

Occasionally you receive event invitations from Facebook friends. These invitations show up in the Events section at the top right of your Home page, as shown in Figure 13.8. Click Yes, No, or Maybe to respond to the invitation or click the event's title to view its Facebook page.

Figure 13.8. *Event notifications on the Facebook Home page.*

You can also receive invitations via regular email. (Not a Facebook private message, but the regular old email address that you supplied to Facebook when you first signed up.) Figure 13.9 shows what an email invitation looks like; click the link in the email to open your web browser and display the event's Facebook page. You can RSVP from there.

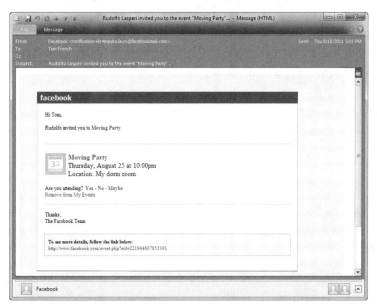

Figure 13.9. *An event invitation sent via email.*

Creating New Events

What if you're hosting an event, be that a block party or family reunion, and want to let friends know about it? It's time now to learn how to create Facebook events—and invite your friends.

Follow these steps:

1. Go to the Facebook Home page, and select Events in the sidebar.

2. From the Events page, click the Create an Event button.

3. When the Create Event page appears, as shown in Figure 13.10, click the controls in the When section to set the start date and time for the event.

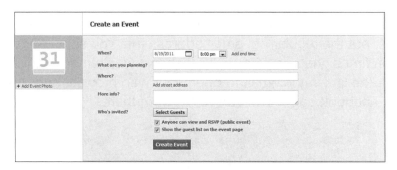

Figure 13.10. *Creating a new Facebook event.*

4. To set the end time for the event, click the Add End Time link to display the End Time section, and then use the controls to set the end date and time.

5. Type the name of the event into the What Are You Planning? box.

6. Type the location of the event into the Where? box.

7. To enter a specific street address, click the Add Street Address link, and then enter the address.

8. Add any additional information about the event into the More Info? box.

9. To invite friends to your event, click the Select Guests button. When the Select Guests dialog box appears, as shown in Figure 13.11, click those Facebook friends you want to invite or enter the email addresses of non-Facebook invitees, and then click the Save and Close button.

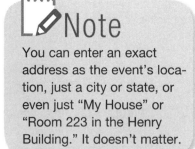

Note

You can enter an exact address as the event's location, just a city or state, or even just "My House" or "Room 223 in the Henry Building." It doesn't matter.

Figure 13.11. *Inviting friends to an event.*

10. Back on the Create Event page, you have the option of making this a public or private event. To make this a public event that all Facebook members can view, check the Anyone Can View and RSVP (Public Event) option. To make this a private event, open to invitees only, uncheck this option.

11. By default, the guest list is displayed on the Event page. Your guests might not always want their presence known; to hide this guest list, uncheck the Show Guest List on the Event Page option.

12. Click the Create Event button.

That's it. You've now created your event and invited some guests. To invite more guests or just monitor who's attending, navigate to the event's Facebook page and do what you need to do there.

Viewing Your Events

Where do you find the pages for those events you've created or have been invited to? All you have to do is go to the Facebook Home page and click the Events link in the sidebar.

This displays the Events page, shown in Figure 13.12, which shows all events to which you've been invited. Your RSVP status—whether you've accepted or declined the invitation—is displayed beside each event listed. To display the Facebook page for an event, click the event title in the list.

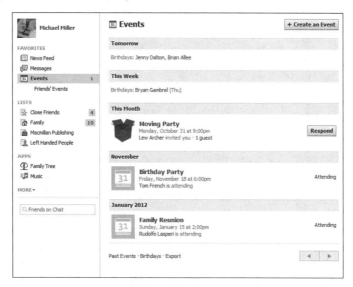

Figure 13.12. *The Facebook Events page.*

And here's something else you might find useful. Many users find that they're interested in events their friends are attending. To display your friends' events, go to the Events page, and click the Friends' Events link in the sidebar. This displays your friend's upcoming events. Click an event title to view its Facebook page—and if you like what you see, RSVP from there.

Celebrating Birthdays

Facebook knows a lot about you and your friends, including when you were born. To that end, Facebook does a nice little social service by letting you know when someone's birthday is nigh.

First off, Facebook notifies you when it's one of your friends' birthday. The notice pops up in the Events section of your Home page, in the top-right corner, as shown in Figure 13.13.

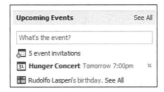

Figure 13.13. *Today's birthdays on your Facebook Home page.*

To get a bit more notice of upcoming birthdays, click the Events link in the sidebar of the Home page to display the Events page, and then scroll down to the bottom of the page and click the Birthdays link. This lists all upcoming birthdays, soonest first, as shown in Figure 13.14.

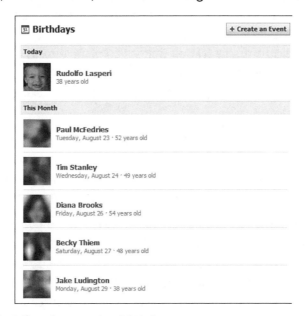

Figure 13.14. *A list of upcoming birthdays.*

And when it's someone's birthday, don't be shy about celebrating. Go to that friend's Profile page and leave them a happy birthday message. It's what people do on Facebook!

Selling Tickets

Facebook's Events feature is a good way to put events on your schedule, but it isn't perfect. Although it's adequate for inviting friends to a private party or letting people know about a big public gathering, it isn't that great when you're hosting an event that requires tickets to get in. That's right, Facebook doesn't let you sell (or give away) tickets to your event.

There's a way around this limitation, however, thanks to Facebook's integration with services like Eventbrite, EventPay, and Social Ticketing. These are services that make it easy to promote and sell tickets for events online. You can connect your Facebook event with the ticketing site, and then use that site to sell tickets to your event. Some of these sites even put "order tickets" links into your News Feed posts for new events. (Most also charge a fee, typically a small percentage of the ticket price.)

You activate these ticketing applications from within Facebook. Just enter the application's name into the search box and you see a link for that app; click the link to go to the application's Facebook page. When you're there, click the Go to App button to get more instructions.

Let's look at Eventbrite as an example of how this all works. After you go to the Eventbrite page and click the Go to App button, you see a long page that contains all the instructions you need to create a new ticketed event. Click the Create an Event button on this page to create an Eventbrite event, complete with ticket information. After you've created the event, Eventbrite invites selected friends to your event and posts an update about the event to Facebook, where it appears in your friends' News Feeds. It's really quite simple.

Chapter 14

Managing Your Facebook Account

Just because you have your Facebook account set up doesn't mean you can't change it. Facebook offers a lot of settings to configure, which can affect the way you use the Facebook site. And, of course, you might need to change bits and pieces of your profile if things change in your life.

Changing Account Settings

Your Facebook account contains your basic personal information—your name, email address, password, and the like. What do you do if you change your name after a divorce (or remarriage), get a new email account, or find that your password is compromised? Fortunately, Facebook lets you easily change all of these items.

All you have to do is click the down arrow on the Facebook toolbar, and then select Account Settings. This displays the Account Settings page, which has seven different tabs. I describe what's on each tab and why you might want to edit those settings.

General

The General tab on the Account Settings page, as shown in Figure 14.1, is where you edit most of your basic account information. What information are we talking about? Here's what you find on the General tab:

Account Settings

Name	Michael Miller	Edit
Username	http://www.facebook.com/**molehillgroup**	Edit
Email	Primary: **mmiller@molehillgroup.com**	Edit
Password	Password last changed over a year ago.	Edit
Networks	No networks.	Edit
Linked Accounts	You have linked **0 linked accounts**.	Edit
Language	English (US)	Edit

Download a copy of your Facebook data.

Figure 14.1. *Managing your General Account Settings.*

- **Name.** You can change your first, middle, and last names, as well as enter an alternate name (like a nickname) you'd rather go by. You can also select how you want your name displayed—first name first or last name first.

- **Username.** This is a little different from a nickname. A Facebook username actually affects the URL, or web address, of your Facebook Profile page. If you choose to enter a username, that username becomes your Facebook address. For example, if you choose the username "bobbysmith," your Facebook URL is www.facebook.com/bobbysmith. The problem with usernames is that all the good ones are probably already taken; if Facebook tells you a username is not available, try again.

- **Email.** This is the email address that Facebook uses to contact you. You can enter more than one address and specify a given address as the main contact. You can also remove old or unused email addresses

 **Tip**

If you're a woman and have been married at least once but you still want your high school friends to find you on Facebook, change your middle name on the Facebook site to include your maiden name—and any other married names you've collected previous to your current one. So, for example, if you were Tammy Smith in high school but are Tammy Borgendorfer now, you should call yourself Tammy Smith Borgendorfer on Facebook. This way anyone searching Facebook for Tammy Smith can still find you.

and change your Facebook email address. The only thing is you have to have at least one email address on file with Facebook, so they can contact you if need be. You don't have to display this address, of course; that's determined by your Facebook privacy settings, as I discuss in Chapter 15, "Keeping Some Things Private: Managing Facebook's Privacy Settings."

Tip

If the obvious usernames are taken, try using alternatives such as "bobby.smith," "bobby-smith," "bobby-smith2010," and so forth.

- **Password.** You can, at any time, change the password you use to log in to Facebook. This is recommended if you think someone has guessed your password. Heck, it's good security to change your password periodically, just to keep the bad guys guessing.

- **Networks.** If you're a member of any school or work networks, they're listed here. Click the Join Another Network link to add new networks to your account.

- **Linked Accounts.** Facebook lets you link your Facebook account with other accounts you might have at the following sites and services: Google, MySpace, Yahoo!, MyOpenID, Verisign PIP, and OpenID. If you log in to one of these other sites and services, you are automatically logged in to Facebook, as well.

- **Language.** Want to view Facebook in a language other than English? Then make a selection in this section; at present, you can view Facebook in everything from Afrikaans to Turkish and just about anything in-between.

Tip

There's also a link on the General tab to Download a Copy of Your Facebook Data. This downloads your photos and videos, your posts and chat conversations, and some (not all) of your friends' names and email addresses—perfect for archiving on your computer or uploading to another social network.

To change a given setting, click the Edit link to the right of that item. This changes the page to display the relevant information for that item. For example, when you click the Edit link for the Name setting, the page changes to that in Figure 14.2, with boxes First Name, Middle Name, Last Name, and Alternate Name, as well as a pull-down list to select how you want your name displayed (Display As). Each item on this page has its own unique information boxes for you to work with.

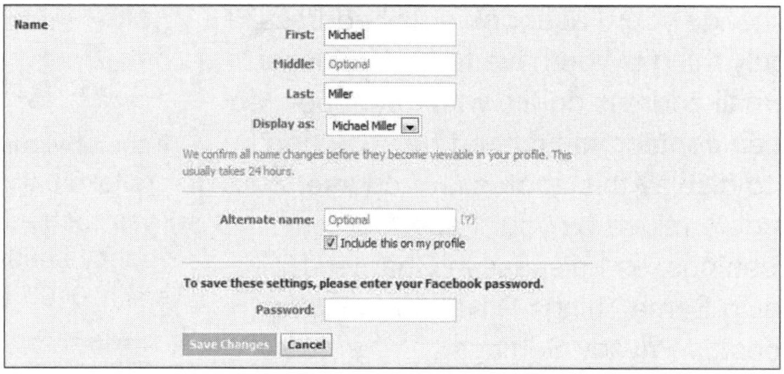

Figure 14.2. *Changing your name.*

Security

The Security Settings tab, as shown in Figure 14.3, contains several settings that can help make your Facebook use a little more secure. Here's what you find:

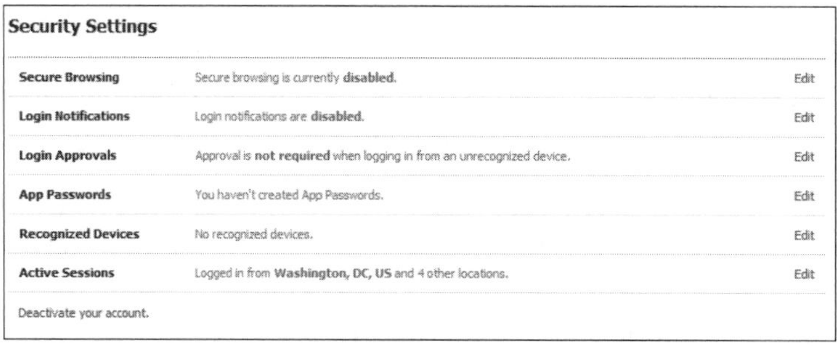

Figure 14.3. *Editing Security settings.*

- **Secure Browsing.** When you enable this option, you access Facebook over a secure https: connection, when available. This is probably security overkill; secure connections are necessary when transmitting personal information when you're making a purchase online, but not really for updating your Facebook status.

- **Login Notifications.** Enable this option to have Facebook notify you (via email) if your account is accessed from a computer or mobile device you haven't used before.

- **Login Approvals.** Enable this option to have Facebook require a security code to be entered if you try to log in from an unrecognized computer or mobile device.

- **App Passwords.** Lets you create passwords for using selected Facebook apps.

- **Recognized Devices.** Speaking of recognized devices, if you have any they're listed here.

Note

Don't confuse security with privacy. Facebook offers a lot of privacy settings, which you learn about in Chapter 15.

- **Active Sessions.** Select this option to view your last few logons, displaying when and where you logged on from. This might not be totally useful, especially if you're accessing Facebook from a public hotspot that might route its access through another server in a totally different location.

This page is also where you can deactivate (but not delete) your Facebook account. Go to the "Leaving Facebook" section, later in this chapter, to learn more.

Notifications

The Notifications Settings tab displays recent notifications you've received from the Facebook site, as well as options that tell Facebook when you want to be notified about what.

As you've probably noticed, Facebook likes to send you a lot of notifications—more than you might like. You get emails when someone sends you a message, adds you as a friend, confirms a friend request, tags you in a post, tags you in a photo, comments on a photo in which you were tagged, invites you to an event, and more. As I said, lots of messages.

Fortunately, you can control which of these events triggers a message from Facebook—and whether you receive that message via email or on your mobile phone. Just scroll to the All Notifications section of the Notifications Settings tab, shown in Figure 14.4, and click the Edit link next to the particular item or activity listed. You can set general Facebook notifications, as well as notifications related to photos, groups, pages, events, and so forth. Just toggle a given notification on or off by checking or unchecking that notification's check box.

All Notifications			
Facebook		✉ 4	Edit
Photos		✉ 2	Edit
Groups		✉ 1	Edit
Pages		✉ 1	Edit
Events			Edit
Questions			Edit
Notes		✉ 1	Edit
Links			Edit
Video		✉ 1	Edit
Help Center			Edit
Wall Comments			Edit
Places		✉ 1	Edit
Deals		✉ 1	Edit

Figure 14.4. *Managing Facebook notifications.*

By default, you receive notifications via email. If you've entered your mobile phone information, you also have the option of receiving notifications via SMS (text message). Select which method you prefer for each notification.

Applications

Click the Apps tab to manage all the third-party applications that interact with your Facebook account. As you can see in Figure 14.5, there are probably a lot of them. This tab lists all the apps you've used, the most recent ones first.

Click the Edit button next to an app to tell Facebook what this app can do and who this app can share information with. As you can see in Figure 14.6, different apps can request different levels of access; some apps want to access your information, post to your Wall, and share your information with friends and more.

Tip

Facebook likes to send you a lot of notifications, even about activities that you probably don't care that much about. Be sure you work through all the various items in the All Notifications section to reduce the number of notifications Facebook sends you—and to make sure you only get notified about what's important to you.

Note

What's an application? Learn more in Chapter 20, "Finding Fun Games and Applications."

Application Settings

You have authorized these apps to interact with your Facebook account:

DISQUS Comments [reefbuilders]	Less than 24 hours ago	Edit ×
CNN Social	August 15	Edit ×
Quora	August 12	Edit ×
Pandora	August 3	Edit ×
Clicker.com	August 2	Edit ×
Ticketmaster	August 1	Edit ×
Spotify	July 29	Edit ×
Bing	July 28	Edit ×
Amplify	July 24	Edit ×
ShareThis	July 21	Edit ×
Urbanspoon	July 19	Edit ×
Foursquare	July 12	Edit ×
Skype	July 7	Edit ×

Figure 14.5. *Managing application access.*

Figure 14.6. *Viewing settings for the Pandora application.*

This is a tricky one, as by default most apps want to share all your information with everyone on the Facebook site. That's not necessarily a good thing; you end up with Facebook serving up ads to your friends that make it look like you've endorsed the particular application, as well as all sorts of pointless status updates in your friend's feed whenever you use the app.

I talk more about this in Chapter 15, but you might want to customize certain apps so that they *don't* share information with your friends. In most cases, they don't need to; it's strictly a marketing thing which results in bit of invasion of everyone's privacy. Configure these settings intelligently.

You can also delete any application you're not using. Just click the X to the right of that application's name, and it isn't around to bother you (or your friends) any more.

Mobile

If you want Facebook to send text messages to your phone, click the Messages tab. As you can see in Figure 14.7, all your mobile settings are displayed here. You can view all your registered phones, as well as edit your text messaging, notifications, Facebook Mobile, and daily text limit settings.

Figure 14.7. *Managing mobile settings.*

Payments

Some apps and games use a currency called Facebook Credits to buy things online. You can manage your Facebook Credits and payments settings by clicking the Payments tab, as shown in Figure 14.8.

Note

Learn more about Facebook's mobile functionality in Chapter 22, "Using Facebook on the Go."

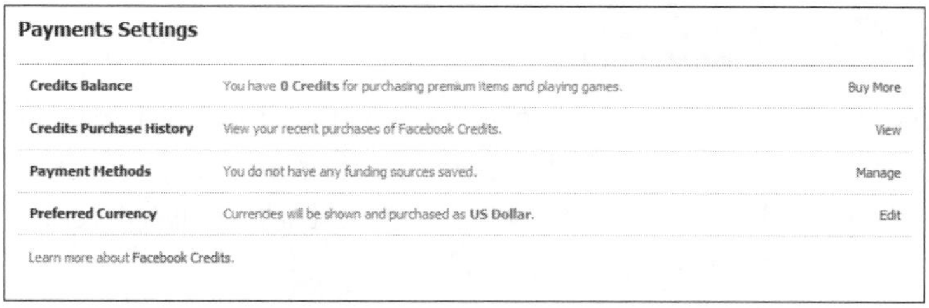

Payments Settings

Credits Balance	You have **0 Credits** for purchasing premium items and playing games.	Buy More
Credits Purchase History	View your recent purchases of Facebook Credits.	View
Payment Methods	You do not have any funding sources saved.	Manage
Preferred Currency	Currencies will be shown and purchased as **US Dollar.**	Edit

Learn more about **Facebook** Credits.

Figure 14.8. *Managing Facebook payments and currency.*

Facebook Ads

Finally, the Facebook Ads tab, as shown in Figure 14.9, lets you edit the way your personal information is used in Facebook ads. Click the Edit Third Party Ad Settings link to permit your name or picture to be shown in ads to your friends or to no one.

Then there are so-called "social ads" that Facebook displays on your friends' pages—the ones that make it look like you're endorsing a given product or brand. (Your name typically appears as "John Smith likes this.") Click the Edit Social Ads Setting link to allow your name to be used in these ads on your friends pages or not.

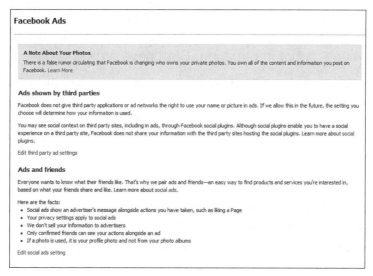

Figure 14.9. *Managing how Facebook uses your name and picture in ads.*

Leaving Facebook

It happens. You give Facebook a spin but find it's just not for you. Maybe you're just not interested. Maybe you're *too* interested and find it consuming too much of your time. Maybe you discover that none of your real friends and family members are using the site.

Whatever the case, you want to leave Facebook. Unfortunately, leaving is not that easy to do. Facebook does such a good job of networking people that it's difficult to leave your friends behind; if you leave Facebook, how do you keep in touch with all your Facebook friends?

Even if you think you can live without a constant barrage of Facebook status updates, figuring out how to delete your Facebook account isn't that terribly easy to do. Facebook does a pretty good job of hiding what you need to use to permanently erase your presence from the Facebook site.

How can you remove your account from Facebook? There are two ways to do it, and I show you both.

Deactivating Versus Deleting

As a Facebook user, you have two options for leaving the Facebook fold. You can *deactivate* your account, which temporarily hides your account information from others, or you can *delete* your account, which permanently removes your account information. Both have pros and cons.

Deactivating your account is meant as a temporary solution. That is, it's something that can be undone. When you deactivate your account, Facebook doesn't actually delete your account information; it merely hides it so others can't view it. Out of sight, out of mind, I suppose; you're not really gone.

Because your account information still exists, it's simple enough to reactivate a deactivated account. This makes deactivation the preferred method if you think you might want to rejoin the Facebook fold at some point in the future. Of course, it also means that all your account information is still sitting on Facebook's servers, just waiting for somebody to use it in some fashion. (Facebook, for its part, says it won't share deactivated data, but since when do you trust ginormous profit-oriented corporations?)

If you're absolutely, positively sure you'll never want to be a Facebook user again—and you want more reassurance that your personal data has been wiped—then you want to permanently delete your account. This is more difficult to do, for the simple reason that your Facebook account is likely connected to lots of other websites. To erase your presence from the Facebook site, you also need to sever all these external connections to your Facebook account. But after you do that, you can leave Facebook free and clear—without fear of being sucked back into the network in the future.

Deactivating Your Account

Let's start, then, with the less-permanent approach of deactivating your Facebook account. It's a surprisingly simple process, if you know where to click.

Here's how to do it:

1. Log in to your Facebook account.

2. Click the down arrow in the Facebook toolbar, and select Account Settings.

3. On the Account Settings page, select the Security tab.

4. Scroll to the bottom of the Security tab, and click the Deactivate Your Account link.

5. Here's where it gets tough. As you can see in Figure 14.10, Facebook really, really doesn't want to see you leave, so it tugs at your heartstrings by showing you pictures of some of your Facebook friends with the messages "Bob will miss you," "Dinah will miss you," and so forth. Resist the urge to change your mind.

6. Scroll to the Reason for Leaving section, and select just why it is you're leaving. This is a requirement; you have to tell Facebook something here.

7. If you have any Facebook Groups, you need to check each group to close it.

8. If you don't want to be hounded by Facebook to venture back into the fold, check the Opt Out of Receiving Future Emails from Facebook box.

9. If you've developed any applications, check the Permanently Delete All Applications for Which I'm the Only Developer box.

10. Click the Confirm button.

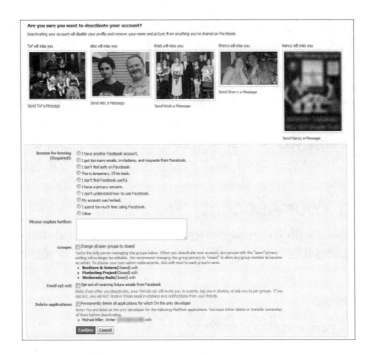

Figure 14.10. *Deactivating your Facebook account—if you can resist the pleas to stay.*

Facebook now hides your account from other Facebook users. However, you retain the option of reactivating your account at any time—and Facebook still has all your personal information on file, for what it's worth.

Deleting Your Account

If you really, really want to leave Facebook—forever—then you need to delete your entire account. This is a more difficult, but not impossible, process, because you have to sever all connections between your Facebook account and other websites.

Don't have any connections between Facebook and other sites? Think again. Any site you've visited that has prompted you to log in with your Facebook information, any site where you've shared something to your Facebook profile, or any site that you've "liked" to Facebook is connected to your Facebook account. These are officially called Facebook Connect sites, and Facebook has done a good job encouraging the participation of thousands of other sites in this extended social network.

What you need to do is visit each of your personal Facebook Connect sites—especially those where you've been logging in with your Facebook account—and establish a different login method. After you delete your Facebook account, you are no longer able to log in to these sites with your old Facebook account, so you want to make sure you can get in afterward. Practically, this probably means logging in with your Facebook account, and then after you're in the site, changing your login information to something different.

This is also important because you can still log in to these connected sites with your Facebook account info for two weeks after you've deleted your Facebook account. In spite of what you might think, this is not a good thing; if you log in to a Facebook Connect website, you actually *undelete* your newly deleted account and have to start over with the deletion process. Better to do your homework ahead of time.

After you've disconnected from all connected sites, you can formally delete your Facebook account. Here's how to do it:

1. Log in to your Facebook account.

2. Go to www.facebook.com/help/contact.php?show_form=delete_account. You have to enter this URL directly into your web browser; there's no link (that I've been able to find, anyway) to this page from within Facebook.

3. When you see the Delete My Account page, as shown in Figure 14.11, click the Submit button.

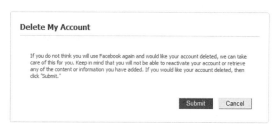

Figure 14.11. *Deleting your Facebook account—permanently.*

4. You now see the Permanently Delete Account dialog box, as shown in Figure 14.12. Enter your Facebook password and the characters in the Security Check box.

Figure 14.12. *Are you really, truly sure you want to delete your account?*

5. Click the Okay button.

That's it. Facebook now deletes your account—as long as you don't log back into Facebook for the next 14 days. (In fact, Facebook sends you an email to this effect.) Any interaction with your Facebook account during this 14-day period reactivates your account.

So you should make sure you do the following:

*   *Do not* log in to your Facebook account.

*   *Do not* log in to any Facebook Connect sites using your Facebook account.

*   *Do not* click the Facebook Share or Like buttons on any websites you visit.

After two weeks, you should be in the clear, and your account should be permanently deleted. Bye-bye, Facebook!

Why You Need to Check Your Settings

I know from experience that this is the chapter most users tend to flip past. Why bother with the boring stuff about configuring your account settings? Everything's set up all ready, there's nothing to change—right?

Wrong.

You see, you might not have changed anything, but Facebook probably has. Facebook changes more often than any website I've ever dealt with. And it's not just minor stuff, either; Facebook likes to fool around with important stuff, like how it uses your personal information and how often it contacts you. If you're not watching (and you're probably not), Facebook is apt to make some major changes to your privacy and security settings.

Now, I get to the privacy settings in the next chapter, but my advice still stands. Take some time once a month or so to review all the settings on your Account Settings and Privacy Settings pages. Don't assume that everything is always the same or that Facebook notifies you if it wants to change something. Things change, and Facebook probably won't tell you. That's the way it plays the game.

Which means you need to stay on top of every single setting Facebook has—and there are a lot of them, as you've seen. In fact, I'd expect the settings you see to be a little different than the ones I describe in this book; that's how much Facebook likes to change things. Just go to your various settings pages, click through the options, and make sure you agree with all the settings there. Don't be surprised if you find something new or different—and don't be shy about changing stuff you don't like.

Keeping Some Things Private: Managing Facebook's Privacy Settings

Facebook is not a paragon of privacy. It's a *social* network, after all, and being social means sharing of oneself. In Facebook's case, it also means sharing all your personal information by default—which is certainly one way to network with others.

Unfortunately, all this sharing poses a problem for those of us who'd prefer to maintain some semblance of a private life. If you share everything with everyone, then all sorts of information can get out—and be seen by people you don't want seeing it. It's a bit of a challenge, and ultimately it involves a degree of compromise to maintain a social profile while protecting your personal privacy.

Understanding Facebook Privacy

Facebook is all about connecting users to one another. That's how the site functions, after all, by encouraging "friends" and all sorts of public sharing of information.

You can understand why Facebook operates in this fashion. The powers that be think they can better connect users with one another and build a stronger community, by making public all of a user's likes and dislikes. After all, how can you connect to others if you don't know anything about them?

I admit all this makes some degree of sense in the abstract; the more we know about each other, the more likely we are to find people to interact with. But Facebook might take this openness a tad too far.

That's because Facebook, by default, shares all your information with just about everybody. Not just your friends or friends of your friends, but the entire membership of the site. And not just with Facebook members, either; Facebook also shares your information with third-party applications and games and with other sites on the Web.

Do you really want your personal information and Facebook status updates shared with millions of strangers and hundreds of thousands of unrelated websites? I think most people would say no, but this is precisely what Facebook now does—unless you specify otherwise.

So, by default, Facebook tries to link all sorts of things together. It shares your Facebook data with partner websites, in the guise of helping those sites "personalize" their content for you. It shares your name with entertainers and companies you say you like to help them "connect" with you as a fan. And it shares your personal information and the posts you make to everyone on the Facebook site, even if you'd rather keep that information private.

Fortunately, you can configure Facebook to be much less public than it is by default. Although this originally was somewhat difficult to do (Facebook didn't put all the settings in the same place—or make them easy to find, for that matter), Facebook has made some changes that make it a trifle easier to control which people and what applications can see your personal information.

Note

This sharing with other websites is part of Facebook's Open Graph protocol, which helps other sites link to the Facebook site. This can come in the form of a common sign-in (you log in to the other site using your Facebook ID and password), a Facebook "like" button on the other site, or the wholesale sharing of information about you between the two sites.

Note

Why does Facebook encourage this wholesale sharing of your private information? It's all about Facebook's apparent quest for world domination. Facebook wants to be your gateway to the Internet, your home page on the Web, or let's be honest, your entire online operating system. Nice for it; less so for you or anyone who values her online privacy.

Controlling Your Default Privacy

Most of Facebook's privacy settings can be accessed from a single gateway page. Not all settings are on this page, but you can get to them from here.

To display the Privacy Settings page, as shown in Figure 15.1, click the down arrow on the Facebook toolbar and select Privacy Settings. The page you see leads you to pretty much everything privacy-related on the site.

Figure 15.1. *Facebook's Privacy Settings gateway page.*

The most important part of this page is the Control Your Default Privacy section. Here you have three options for how everything you post and share on Facebook is viewed by default. This setting applies to those status updates and photos you post and upload; this is the default setting you see.

You have three options:

- **Public.** In Facebook parlance, public means "everybody." Select this option, and everything you post is visible to everyone on Facebook.

- **Friends.** This one's easy to understand. Select this option, and everything you post is visible to everyone on your friends list—but to no one else.

- **Custom.** Select this option to select specific people who can view your content or specific people who can't view it. You can also use the Custom option to forbid sharing with anyone except yourself.

Check the sharing option you want, and it is applied throughout the Facebook site.

Setting Custom Sharing Options

The Public and Friends options are easy enough to understand, but what about that Custom option?

Remember, you can also determine who can view your status updates on a post-by-post basis. When you enter a new status update, click the Sharing button (down arrow) beneath the text box; click this to display the privacy menu of Public, Friends, or Custom. Make your selection and this particular post is only viewable by the group you select.

The Custom option is great for when you really want to fine-tune your sharing options on a very granular basis. Don't want to share your photos with all your friends? Don't want to share your contact information with *anyone*? That's what the Custom option is for.

When you select the Custom option for any privacy setting (including the default setting just discussed), you see the Custom Privacy dialog box, as shown in Figure 15.2. From here you can do the following:

Figure 15.2. *Customizing Facebook's privacy settings.*

- To hide an item from everyone, pull down the Make This Visible To list and select Only Me.

- To make an item visible only to specific people, pull down the Make This Visible To list, select Specific People or Lists, and then enter the names of those Facebook users (or the name of a custom friends list) you want to see the info.

> **Tip**
>
> If you're a member of a company or school network, you'll also have the option of making an item visible to or hiding it from members of that network.

- To hide an item only from specific people, enter their names into the Hide This From These People box. (This is a good way to hide specific info from your boss or spouse—or your kids.)

Remember to click the Save Setting button when done.

Controlling How You Connect

How much of your personal information can people see on Facebook? And just who can contact you on the Facebook site—and how? You can control all the connections with other Facebookers.

Go to the How You Connect section of the Privacy Settings page, and click Edit Settings. This displays the How You Connect dialog box, as shown in Figure 15.3. There are five settings here you can configure:

Figure 15.3. *Controlling who can connect with you on Facebook.*

- **Who can look up your profile by name or contact info?** This controls who can find you on Facebook. The options are Everyone, Friends of Friends, or Friends.

- **Who can send you friend requests?** In other words, who can ask to be your friend? The options are Everyone or Friends of Friends.

- **Who can send you Facebook messages?** This controls who can contact you privately on the Facebook site. The options are Everyone, Friends of Friends, or Friends.

- **Who can post on your timeline?** Remember, posts made to the timeline on your Profile page are public postings. The options here are Friends or Only Me. (Select Only Me to forbid anyone from posting on your Wall.)

- **Who can see posts by others on your timeline?** That is, who can read the public posts on your Profile page made by others? The options are Public, Friends of Friends, Friends, Only Me, Custom, or any custom friends lists you or Facebook have created.

Click the Done button when you're done making your selections.

Controlling How Tags Work

If you want more control over what happens when someone tags you in a photo or tags someone else in one of your photos, go to the How Tags Work section of the Privacy Settings page, and click Edit Settings. When the How Tags Work dialog box appears, as shown in Figure 15.4, you can work with these settings:

Figure 15.4. *Configuring tag-related options.*

- **Timeline Review.** Enable Timeline Review to approve or reject all posts in which you're tagged before they're displayed on your Profile.

- **Tag Review.** Enable Tag Review to approve or reject tags that friends might want to add to your posts.

- **Maximum Timeline Visibility.** This determines who can see photos, videos, and other posts in which you're tagged on your Profile. The options are Public, Friends of Friends, Friends, Custom, or any custom friends lists you or Facebook have created.

! Caution

Even if you enable Timeline Review and reject a tag, the post is still made—it just doesn't appear on your Profile page.

- **Tag Suggestions.** When enabled, Facebook uses its face recognition technology to identify your face in photos uploaded by others and suggests tagging you.

- **Friends Can Check You into Places.** When this option is enabled, your friends can check you into locations using Facebook Mobile Places. Disable this option to retain some small semblance of privacy while you're out and about.

Make your changes, and then click the Done button.

Controlling What Gets Shared with Apps and Other Websites

One big concern I have with Facebook is how much of my information it shares with other websites. Facebook is on a drive, it seems, to connect everybody with everything and that means sharing as much information as possible with other sites—which is something not everyone is comfortable with.

So here's a simple way to make sure Facebook doesn't share your information with other websites: Don't log in to these sites with your Facebook account! That's right; if a website doesn't know you're on Facebook or who you are on Facebook, it can't link to your Facebook account. So when you go to a site and you're prompted to use your Facebook ID to log in, just don't do it. Use your normal ID for that site instead—and if you don't yet have an ID, establish one separate from your Facebook ID.

There's more. If, when you visit a website, you see a blue bar at the top of the page informing you that this site is using Facebook "to personalize your experience," you also see a "No Thanks" link in the bar. Click "No Thanks" and the site doesn't use your Facebook data.

In addition, you can configure Facebook to turn off this data-sharing feature—as well as configure other settings related to apps and third-party websites. Just open the Privacy Settings page, go to the Apps and Websites section, and then click the Edit Settings link. This displays the Apps, Games and Websites page shown in Figure 15.5.

Figure 15.5. *Configuring settings for apps, games, and third-party websites.*

From here you can do the following:

- **Apps you use.** Click the Edit Settings button here to display the App Settings page, from which you can delete or manage the settings for the various apps you use on Facebook.

Note

We discussed the Application Settings page in Chapter 14, "Managing Your Facebook Account." Turn there for more information.

- **How people bring your info to apps they use.** Click the Edit Settings button in this section to determine which of your personal information your friends can bring to the apps that they use. This includes your bio, birthday, family and relationships, photos, videos—you name it. The less info you let friends share, the more protected your privacy; the more info you let them share, the more social your experience on Facebook.

- **Instant personalization.** You might not know this, but Facebook likes to share your personal information (including who your friends are) with select third-party websites, such as Pandora and TripAdvisor. Click the Edit Settings button to disable what some feel is a real invasion of your personal privacy.

- **Public search.** If you want Facebook to feed your name and profile information to various search engines, so people searching for you on the Web can find you, do nothing; that's the default status. However, if you'd rather not be found by strangers searching the Web, click the Edit Settings button to disable this public search.

Limiting Who Can See Old Posts

By default, old information you've shared publicly on Facebook stays public. If you'd rather limit the availability of this information going forward, Facebook can limit the audience for these old posts to just your friends; go to the Limit the Audience for Past Posts section of the Privacy Settings page, and click the Manage Past Post Visibility link. When the next dialog box appears, click the Limit Old Posts button.

Managing Your Block Lists

In Chapter 7, "Organizing Groups of Friends," we talked about how to block people from contacting you on Facebook. Well, you can manage these lists of blocked users from the Blocked People and Lists section of the Privacy Settings page. Just click the Manage Block Lists link to do what you need to do.

Protecting Your Kids—and Grandkids—on Facebook

It's not just your own personal information you have to worry about on Facebook. If you have younger children or grandchildren online, you should be concerned about how they use the site and what information they share.

Here's the thing with younger folks on Facebook: They tend to be very open about their lives, wanting to share just about everything with everyone. Although you might have a few dozen friends, your kids might have hundreds of friends. Now, they don't know all these people personally, but they share all their innermost thoughts and personal information with them, anyway—and they think nothing of it.

The problem is everything that can come back to bite you about Facebook can hurt your kids, too. An ill-advised post about a hated teacher could put your child in hot water in school. A gripe about a boss can cost your child his part-time job. A nasty comment about another kid can result in an online flame war—or something worse.

And, speaking of worse, check out some of the photos your kids and their friends post online. Yes, they're ignorant enough to upload pictures of themselves doing all sorts of stupid, unethical, and sometimes illegal stuff. Drinking, smoking, drugs, or sex—kids don't think twice about posting all sorts of compromising pictures. Not very smart of them, but then, how smart were you at that age?

The point is you need to monitor what your kids do online and steer them away from the most damaging behavior. You probably can't keep them from making dumb posts, but you can discourage them from doing so—and, hopefully, delete offending posts or incriminating photos after the fact. Kids will be kids, after all, and there's only so much monitoring you can do.

But that's not the only thing you need to be concerned about, especially with younger kids. Facebook can be home to dangerous predators, who use the site to befriend victims. There's no proof that the 13-year-old girl on your child's friends list is actually a 13-year-old girl; it could a 40-year-old male predator, and you'd never know.

To that point, you should stress to your kids the dangers of meeting up with anonymous "friends" from Facebook. It's okay to share messages online, but when it comes to meeting in the real world, extreme caution is called for. Your kids need to know that people aren't always who they say they are online and that real dangers exist out in the world. They should never, *ever* arrange for an unescorted real-world meeting with a Facebook friend they've never seen in person before. If they insist on meeting up with an unknown "friend," make sure it's in a public place and be there yourself to supervise the meeting. Your children's safety is paramount, and no amount of social networking should get in the way of that.

Chapter 16

What to Say—and What *Not* to Say—Online

In all this discussion about Facebook privacy and security, we can't lay all the responsibility on Facebook's shoulders. Yes, Facebook has a responsibility to keep its users' communications secure and relatively private, and it offers a variety of settings to help do so, but at the end of the day Facebook can't protect us from ourselves. That is, we all have some degree of personal responsibility when posting on Facebook and other social networking sites.

You can do a lot of damage to yourself by posting something stupid. And people post stupid, harmful stuff all the time. It's like some folks forget that Facebook is a *public* forum, not a private one; everything you post can and probably will become public—and ultimately come back to haunt you.

All of which is why you need to be careful what you post on Facebook.

How Private Is Your Information on Facebook?

Many of the potential hazards of social networking revolve around personal information posted publicly. Because Facebook encourages you to enter some degree of private information about yourself, it's possible that some or all of this information doesn't remain private.

Keeping Private Information Private

Of first concern is the information in your Facebook profile. As you've learned, Facebook requires certain information, such as your email address, and encourages you to enter additional information, such as your postal address and phone number. Fortunately, you have the option of hiding most of this information, as you learned in Chapter 15, "Keeping Some Things Private: Managing Facebook's Privacy Settings." You should use this knowledge to hide as much personal information as possible from as many people as possible.

The other private information that might become public is anything you might post as part of your regular status updates—what you did last night, who you're seeing, or what you think of your teacher or boss. These posts are typically public by default, which means that anyone can read them. As with the information on your Profile page, however, you can employ Facebook's update-specific Privacy Settings to limit who can see the information in any given post. In this fashion, you can avoid full public disclosure of your private life if you so choose.

How Facebook Uses Your Personal Information

When it comes to keeping private information private, we naturally think about the outside threats to our privacy and safety. But there's another threat, and it comes directly from Facebook. That's because the personal information you provide to Facebook can be used in a number of ways—not all of which are to your benefit.

For example, Facebook can use your profile information—age, gender, education, and so forth—to display targeted third-party advertisements on your Home page. These targeted ads might be marginally more appealing than generic advertisements, but are still, at least to some, a violation of your privacy; Facebook uses your own likes and dislikes for the company's benefit to sell advertising.

Similarly, your profile information can be used for targeted invitations of various sorts. For example, Facebook might determine your interests from your profile data and invite you to play a particular game, use a certain application, join a given group, or add someone as a friend. These might appear to be helpful invitations, but still rely on the use of your private information.

It's also possible that Facebook might sell your personal information to interested third parties. After Facebook sells the data to a particular company, you typically receive one or more email messages advertising that company's wares. This isn't spam; you no doubt implicitly agreed that Facebook could share this data when you okayed the site's Terms of Service, and these are legitimate marketers. But it's still an annoying use or abuse of your private information.

All of these uses of your private information are perfectly legal, and you probably agreed to them—assuming you read the fine print, of course. This points out the necessity of reading Facebook's Terms of Service before you sign up—and not participating if you don't like what you read.

Beyond these legal invasions of your privacy, there are many ways your personal information can be used illegally. These illegal invasions of your privacy can result in everything from spam to identity theft; you can guard against them by limiting the amount of personal information you publicly post on the social network site.

Is It Safe to Use Facebook?

There are potential hazards involved in virtually every online activity, from reading emails to web browsing. Such hazards also exist with the use of social networks, such as Facebook.

What kinds of hazards are we talking about? There are both major and minor ones, including the following:

Note

A *computer virus* is a malicious software program that can cause damage to an infected computer. *Spyware* is a similar but different software program that obtains information from your computer without your knowledge or consent. Both viruses and spyware are forms of *malware*, which is short for malicious software.

- **Computer viruses and other malware.** Like any website, a social networking site like Facebook can contain links to computer viruses, spyware, and other forms of malware. If you click on a bad link, often disguised as a link to an interesting website or application, you can infect your computer with this type of malicious software.

- **Spam.** Users who publicly post their email addresses on Facebook and other social networking sites can find themselves the target of unwanted junk email, or spam. Spammers harvest email addresses from social networking sites and add these addresses to their email mailing lists for spam messages.

Note

Identity theft is a form of fraud in which one person pretends to be someone else, typically by stealing personal information, such as a bank number, credit card number, or Social Security number. The intent of identity theft is often to steal money or obtain other benefits.

- **Identity theft.** Posting other personal information publicly on Facebook or similar sites can result in identity theft. Identity thieves can use this public information to assume a user's identity on the social network or on other websites; to apply for credit cards and loans in the user's name; to legitimize undocumented foreign workers; and to gain access to the user's banking and credit card accounts.

- **Online stalking.** Online stalkers like to follow their victims from one website to another. If granted friend status, these online bullies—often pretending to be someone that they're not— try to become close to you, whether for their own personal enjoyment or to cause you discomfort, embarrassment, or actual harm.

- **Physical stalking or harassment.** Some online predators take their stalking into the physical world. This is facilitated when you post personal information—including phone numbers and home addresses—on Facebook and other social networking sites. This information helps predators physically contact their victims, which can result in harassment or even physical violence.

- **Robbery.** Have you ever posted on Facebook about going out for dinner on a given evening or getting ready to take a long vacation? When you do so, you're telling potential robbers when your home will be empty—and that your belongings are ripe for the taking.

Scary stuff, all of it.

That said, social networking is only as hazardous—or as safe—as you make it. If you post a plethora of personal information, you are less safe than if you are more discreet. If you avoid posting personal details about your life, you are safer from potential attackers or identity thieves than if you post liberally about your activities.

How do you avoid these potential dangers? Well, the only sure way to be completely safe is to cease using Facebook and other social media. Short of that, however, you can network in relative safety by being smart about what you post and what you respond to on the site.

What to Keep Private—and What to Share

With the aforementioned potential hazards in mind, just what should you share on Facebook? What information is best kept private—or at least exposed only to your closest friends?

What and how much personal information to share on Facebook depends to a degree on your personal comfort level and your personal life. But in general, you shouldn't share any information that might prove embarrassing to you or your family or that might compromise your current job or future job prospects.

Naturally, what all this means is going to differ from person to person. If you work for an ultra-conservative boss, for example, you might not want him to know that you're a dyed-in-the-wool liberal. And if all your friends are agnostics, you might not want to publicize that you're a born-again Christian.

But it goes further than that. If you're preaching the "just say no" drug message to your kids, you might not want to list *Cheech & Chong's Up in Smoke* as one of your favorite movies; it might compromise your integrity on the matter just a bit. For that matter, you might want to hide all those photos that show you drinking margaritas on the beach, for both your kids' sake and to ward off any awkward questions from teetotalling employers.

In fact, pictures can be more damaging than words. A picture of you holding a cigarette in your hand could be used by your insurance company to raise your rates. Photos of you partying hardy or just acting goofy can raise doubts about your decision-making abilities. Do you really want your boss or your kids or your ex-husband's lawyer to see you in compromising positions?

The same goes with what you post in status updates. There are stories, some of them true, of careless (and carefree) employees posting about this afternoon's golf game when they were supposed to be home sick from work. Employers can and will keep track of you online, if you're stupid enough to post all your comings and goings.

And it's not just factual stuff. Spouting off your opinions is a common-enough Facebook activity, but some people will disagree with you or take more serious offense. Do you really want to start a flame war over something you posted in haste?

For that matter, it's a really bad idea to use Facebook to criticize your employer, the people you work with, or just people you associate with in the community. Posting about how much you hate your job will eventually get back to your boss, and then you've got a lot of 'splainin' to do, Lucy.

Of course, you have the option of making a given post visible only to those on your Facebook friends list. But while it's tempting to share intimate details with your online friends, think about who these "friends" really are. How many of your social network friends are close, intimate friends? How many are merely acquaintances or just people you work with or went to school with? How many are people you really don't know at all?

And you don't limit your updates to just friends; the updates you make may be visible to *everyone* on the Facebook site. That means that hundreds of millions of people could be reading about how you hate your spouse, or how you cheated the IRS, or how you really feel about your boss and coworkers. It's not hard to imagine how this personal information can come back to haunt you.

Of course, who sees which messages depends on the universal privacy settings you make, as well as the privacy settings selected for each individual post. This is a good reason to use Facebook's friends lists and post to selected lists only.

What you have to remember is that on Facebook, you're not invisible. Facebook is a public community; everything you post might be readable by anyone. Post only that information that is safe enough for your family, friends, and coworkers to read.

You see, on Facebook, discretion is definitely the better part of valor. When in doubt, hide it. Or better still, don't post it or upload it in the first place. It's okay to keep some thoughts to yourself; you don't have to post every little thing you think or that happens to you.

How Much Personal Information Should You Share?

Then there's the issue of your contact information. As noted, Facebook requires you to enter contact information (email address, home address, and such) when you sign up for the site. You do not, however, have to display this information for the rest of the world to see. To keep people from contacting you outside of Facebook, you should opt to display as little contact information as possible. After all, do you really want complete strangers phoning you or showing up at your door? They might, if you make this information public.

Here's what I think: You shouldn't make any contact information public. If someone wants to contact you, they can post on your Profile page or send you a Facebook message. They don't have to contact you via regular email, ring you on the phone, or show up on your doorstep. There are too many nutcases out there. Heck, there's just a lot of people I used to know that I don't want to deal with any more. I don't want to make it easy for these people to get in touch with me. I prefer to keep my distance from them.

Bottom line, then, is this: Be careful about the information you post. It's better to keep most of your personal information private.

Sharing Information with Other Sites

Facebook has a program, called Facebook Connect, that lets other sites on the Web link with Facebook. This typically takes the form of signing in to another site using your Facebook account. When you do so, you link your presence on that site with what you do on Facebook.

On the plus side, linking various accounts with your Facebook account can make your life a little easier. You don't have to log in to multiple sites using different usernames and passwords; just use your Facebook login for all those different sites.

In addition, when you link another site to Facebook, the things you "like" on that site are automatically transferred to your Facebook account. Indicate that you like something or make a comment on that site, and it then appears as a Facebook status update. Pretty cool; you comment once, and then share it with all your Facebook friends.

On the minus side, you're sharing a lot of information with those other sites. When you link accounts, all your Facebook information is accessible by the other site—your status updates, profile information, you name it. And what you do on the other site is also transferred to Facebook, that can use it for its own nefarious purposes.

In other words, when you link to Facebook from another site, what you do and say becomes a little less private and a little more public. And do you really want all your Facebook friends knowing that you just listened to an old Bobby Sherman track on Spotify? (I certainly wouldn't.)

If that doesn't bother you, fine; enjoy the benefits of this type of account linkage. If the thought of even more of your information being put out on the Interwebs bothers you, then think twice about linking your accounts. Maintain separate accounts on separate sites; don't link everything to Facebook.

I try to avoid signing into other sites with my Facebook account. Yes, I know there are benefits and conveniences to doing so. But I prefer to keep as much of my comings and goings as private as possible and linking every-thing to Facebook works against this.

Facebook Do's and Don'ts

When it comes to using Facebook, then, there are some general guidelines you should adhere to. These guidelines help you better fit into the community—and protect yourself from any inherent dangers.

Do These Things

If you want to become a safer and more productive Facebook member, fol-low these tips:

- **Post frequently—but not too frequently.** Facebook is a community, and to be a member of that community you have to actively participate. If you wait too long between posts, people forget that you're there. Conversely, if you post too frequently, that might be perceived as overbearing or annoying. The best frequency is somewhere between once a week and a few times per day—for grown-ups, once every day or two is probably good.

- **Keep your posts short and sweet.** People don't want or expect to read overly long musings on Facebook. Instead, they tend to graze, absorbing the gist of what's posted rather than reading entire missives. On a site like Facebook, that means keeping your posts to no more than a few sentences. If you want to pontificate in more detail, get yourself a blog.

- **Use proper spelling.** Although you don't have to use complete and proper grammar and punctuation (see the next tip), blatant misspellings can mark you as less informed than you might actually be. Take the time to spell things correctly; it's literally the least you can do.

- **Take shortcuts.** Although you should always use proper spelling, you don't have to use full sentences when posting to a social network. In fact, it's okay to use common abbreviations and acronyms, such as BTW (by the way) and LOL (laughing out loud). Casual is good.

- **Link to additional information.** You don't always have space to provide a lot of background information in a status update. Instead, you can link to web pages or blog posts that offer more details.

- **Use friends lists.** Facebook's custom friends lists are a great way to segregate your different social identities online. Create one list for work friends, another for play friends, another for family, and so on—and then filter your posts only to selected lists. In other words, use Facebook's privacy settings to help keep your work and home lives separate.

- **Be discrete.** Remember, Facebook status updates are public for all to read. Post only that information that you'd want your friends (or spouse or employer or children) to read.

- **Be cautious.** You don't have to be paranoid about it, but it helps to assume that there are some dangerous people out there. Don't do anything that would put you in harm's way.

Don't Do These Things

Building on that last tip, you should, in general, avoid posting personal information in any public forum, including Facebook. Here are some specific things you should *avoid* when using Facebook:

- **Don't accept every friend request you receive.** You don't need a thousand friends. It's better to have a smaller number of true friends than a larger number of people you really don't know.

- **Don't assume your Facebook friends are real friends.** When you have hundreds of people on your Facebook friends list, how well do you really know any of them? It's possible that some of the people you call "friends" really aren't the people they present themselves to be. For whatever reason, some people adopt different personas—including fake names and profile pictures—when they're online; it's possible that you're establishing relationships on these social networks that have no basis in reality.

- **Don't post if you don't have anything interesting to say.** Some of the most annoying people on Facebook are those that post their every action and movement. ("I just woke up." "I'm reading my mail." "I'm thinking about having lunch." "That coffee was delicious.") Post if there's something interesting happening, but avoid posting just to be posting. Think about what you like to read about other people and post in a similar fashion.

- **Don't assume that everyone online will agree with you.** Some people use Facebook as a platform for their opinions. Whereas it might be okay to share your opinions with close (that is, non-Facebook) friends, spouting off in a public forum is not only bad form, but it's also a way to incite a flame war—an unnecessary online war of words.

- **Don't post anything that could possibly be used against you.** Want to put your job in jeopardy? Then by all means, you should post negative comments about your workplace or employer. And future employment might be denied if a potential employer doesn't like what he sees in your Facebook posts. (And they will be looking....) As in most things, with social networking, it's better to be safe than sorry; avoid posting overly negative comments that are better kept private.

- **Don't post overly personal information.** Along the same lines, think twice before sharing the intimate details of your private life—including embarrassing photographs. Discretion is a value us older folks should maintain; there's no reason for posting pictures of you falling down drunk at the holiday office party or baring it all on the beach during your last vacation. Leave some of the details to imagination.

- **Don't gripe.** Building on that last tip, the last thing I and lots of others want to find in our News Feeds are your private gripes. Oh, it's okay to grouse and be grumpy from time to time, but don't use Facebook as your personal forum for petty grievances. If you have a personal problem, deal with it. You don't have to share *everything*, you know. Whining gets old really fast.

- **Don't post personal contact information.** As nice as Facebook is for renewing old acquaintances, it can also put you in contact with people you really don't want to be in contact with. So don't make it easy for disreputable people or unwanted old boyfriends to find you offline; avoid posting your phone number, email address, and home address.

- **Don't post your constant whereabouts.** You don't need to broadcast your every movement; thieves don't need to know when your house is empty. It's okay to post where you were after the fact, but keep your current whereabouts private.

- **Don't use Facebook as an online dating service.** Yes, you might meet new friends on Facebook, but use caution about transferring online friendships into the physical world. With that in mind, you should never arrange to meet privately with an online "friend" with whom you've never met in person. It's not unheard of for predators to arrange meetings with unsuspecting victims over a social network. If you must meet an online "friend" in person, take someone else with you and meet in a public place.

In other words, don't post every little detail and thought about everything you do. Keep your private life private. And make public only the most general information that those distant acquaintances you call Facebook friends want or need to know.

Telling People About Yourself

How much personal information you display on Facebook is a source of great debate. Some people fill out each and every box in excruciating detail, choosing to tell everybody everything about themselves; others leave most of the boxes unfilled, choosing to keep their personal lives private.

Just how much personal information should you divulge to your Facebook friends? That depends.

I think it's okay to list your favorite movies and books and such; there's little harm in letting people know what you like to read and watch and listen to. Likewise, it's probably okay to list your past employers and where you went to school and such. This is all relatively public information anyway, plus it's a good way to help the people you used to work and study with find you on Facebook.

That said, you don't want to enter any information that could harm you in terms of job prospects, family relations, and the like. Does a potential employer (who might be a staunch conservative) really need to know that you're a dyed-in-the-wool liberal? Will listing that you like to listen to Bobby Sherman and the Archies poison your chances at a new job—or with a potential suitor, if you're dating? It's hard to say, but I do know that some people will form an opinion of you based on what you like and dislike. Right or wrong, the personal information you list on Facebook could work against you.

Then there's the whole issue of contact information, which really is a lot simpler. Unless you want to encourage old flames and new stalkers, don't list any contact information. Let them send you a Facebook message, but don't encourage contact outside of Facebook. Your less-than-close Facebook friends don't need to call you or drop by your house. Leave the social networking online, where it belongs.

Chapter 17

Personalizing Your Profile Page

Your Profile page is your personal page on Facebook. I'd say it's like a home page, except that Facebook's real Home page is something different. So although your Profile page might be your "home," it's actually a place where all your personal information is stored and displayed for your friends to see.

As such, wouldn't it be nice if you could personalize your Profile page to better reflect your personality? Well, although you can't change the page's colors, background, or how it looks in general, there are some things you *can* personalize. That's what we discuss in this chapter.

What Can You Personalize on Your Profile Page—and Why Would You Want To?

Before we look at what you can personalize on your Profile page, let's take another look at what's actually on the page. As you can see in Figure 17.1, your Profile picture is at the top left, with a variety of informational elements beneath it. This little information section also includes graphics that link to your friends, photos, maps, and so forth.

Figure 17.1. *A typical Profile page.*

Beneath the information section is the meat of the Profile page—your time-line. That is, a listing of all your Facebook activity, in reverse chronological order, including status updates, photo and video uploads, events, you name it. And you can jump to any specific point on the timeline by clicking the lit-eral timeline at the far right side of the page.

Now, most of what you see on your Profile page is set in stone by Facebook. That said, you can change your profile picture, add an image "cover" at the top, edit or remove individual posts, and edit your profile information. So Facebook provides some small amount of control over what people see on your Profile page—let's delve deeper.

Changing Your Profile Picture

Here's something you'll probably end up changing quite a bit over time—the picture you display on your Profile page. Fortunately, Facebook makes it easy to change your Profile picture at any point in time. Here's how to do it:

1. From your Profile page, point to your picture, and click the Edit Profile Picture link that appears. This displays a menu of options: Choose from My Photos, Take a Photo, Upload a Photo, Edit Thumbnail, and Remove Your Picture.

2. To select a picture you've already uploaded, click the Choose from My Photos option. When the Select a Photo dialog box appears, as shown in Figure 17.2, select one of the photos of you, or click View Albums to select a photo from one of your photo albums. When the picture page appears, click the Make Profile Picture link.

Figure 17.2. *Choosing a Facebook photo for your profile picture.*

3. To shoot a new picture from your computer's webcam, click Take a Photo. When the Take a Profile Picture dialog box appears, as shown in Figure 17.3, smile and click the camera button. If you like what you see, click the Set as Profile Picture button.

4. To upload a new photo from your computer, click the Upload a Photo option. When the Choose File to Upload or Open dialog box appears, navigate to and select the picture you want to use, and then click the Open button.

5. To edit the thumbnail version of this photo that appears in Facebook's News Feed, click Edit Thumbnail. When the Edit Thumbnail dialog box appears, as shown in Figure 17.4, click and drag the thumbnail until it looks the way you want, and then click the Save button.

Tip

To remove the current Profile picture without replacing it with a new picture (resulting in Facebook's default shadow head image where your picture should be), point to your Profile picture, click Edit Profile Picture, and then select Remove Your Picture.

Figure 17.3. *Shooting a new profile picture with your webcam.*

Figure 17.4. *Editing the thumbnail version of your Profile picture.*

Adding a Cover to Your Page

By default, your profile picture appears against a blue-tinted background on your Profile page. You can, however, select a background image (called a *cover*) to appear on the top of the page, like the one in Figure 17.5. Here's how to do it:

1. Click the Add a Cover button at the top of your Profile page. A pop-up menu now appears with two options: Choose from My Photos and Upload a Photo.

Figure 17.5. *A Profile page with a cover image.*

2. To select a cover image from those photos you've uploaded to Facebook, click Choose from My Photos. When the Choose from Your Photos dialog box appears, select one of the photos of you, or click View Albums to select a photo from one of your photo albums.

3. To select a photo from your computer, click the Upload a Photo option. When the Choose File to Upload or Open dialog box appears, navigate to and select the picture you want to use, and then click the Open button.

4. You're now prompted to drag to reposition the cover image. Use your mouse to position the image appropriately, and then click the Save Changes button.

To change an existing cover image, hover over the image, and click the Change Cover button.

Hiding, Deleting, and Featuring Status Updates

Your Profile page is really a big timeline of the status updates you've made. That doesn't mean you need to display every single status update, however; if there's an embarrassing update out there, you can choose to hide it.

To hide a status update, hover over the update until you see the Edit or Remove (pencil) button, shown in Figure 17.6. Click this button and then select Hide From Timeline.

Figure 17.6. *Featuring or editing/deleting a status update.*

If a post is particularly embarrassing, you might want to delete it completely. To do this, click the Edit or Remove (pencil) button and select Delete Post.

Finally, you can feature a post on your timeline. (Figure 17.7 shows what a featured post looks like—it stretches across both columns.) To do this, click the Feature on Timeline (star) button for that particular update. To "unfeature" a post, just click the Feature on Timeline button again.

Figure 17.7. *A featured post on your Profile page.*

Viewing and Editing Your Activity Log

Your profile page presents all your Facebook activity in a nice, visually attractive fashion. However, if you want a more straightforward view of what you've done online, you can display Facebook's Activity Log.

As you can see in Figure 17.8, the Activity Log lists every little thing you've done on the Facebook site, from status updates to links to comments to you name it. For each item listed, you can click the down-arrow button to select how this item is displayed on the main Profile timeline—Feature on Timeline, Allow on Timeline, or Hide from Timeline. You can also select who can view this particular item—Public, Friends, Custom, or custom friends lists. You can also click this button to delete this particular item.

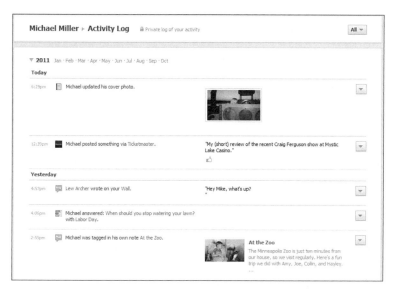

Figure 17.8. *Viewing your Facebook Activity Log.*

Updating Your Profile Information

Then there's the personal information displayed on your Profile page. If you don't like what's there, or need to add to or edit it, you can.

All you have to do is click the Update Info button at the top of your Profile page. This displays the page shown in Figure 17.9. You start by editing the Work and Education section and then click the Done Editing button. Then click the Edit button for any given section, and add/change the appropriate information as necessary.

You can also use this page to select who can view what information in your profile. For example, you might want everyone to view your birthday, but only friends to view your marital status, and no one to view your contact information. You can fine-tune your profile as granularly as you like, in this fashion.

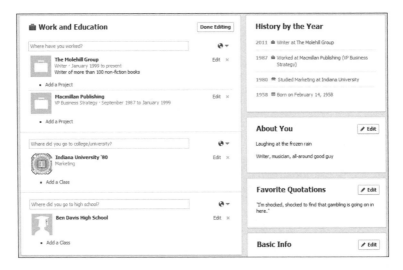

Figure 17.9. *Editing your profile information.*

Just click the privacy button to the right of each item on the editing page. You can select from the following options:

- **Public** (everybody on Facebook)
- **Friends** (only people on your Facebook friends list)
- **Only Me** (nobody but you can see it)
- **Custom** (use to select specific people to view or hide this item from)

You can also opt to have a given piece of information visible only to a selected friends list. Go at it!

Loving the Timeline

Facebook's Profile pages are a lot different than they used to be. In the past, a Profile page displayed a bit of personal information, and that's about it. The move to the timeline approach changes pretty much everything you know about Profile pages.

Facebook's intent is to help you tell the story of your life on a single page. Well, as much of your life as you tell Facebook about, anyway. That might sound like a great thing to you, or it might sound like an incredible invasion of your privacy. I'm probably somewhere in the middle—I appreciate having everything in one place, but I'm not sure I want everyone I know to be able to figure out that much about my life that easily.

That said, the new timeline view makes it quite obvious just how much Facebook knows about each and every one of its 750 million users. Facebook has collected an incredible database of personal information— our likes, dislikes, opinions, tastes, friends, and more. If you get a little queasy about that, you're not alone.

But that's what participating in a social network is all about, I guess. You have to make certain aspects of your personal life public to share socially. If you don't like that, then quit Facebook now—before you get too involved.

Chapter 18

Liking Public Pages

Do you like a given entertainer? I mean, do you really, really like him? Well, on Facebook you can "like" a celebrity in a way that lets you become a kind of friend of that person, receiving his status updates in your News Feed and letting you participate in discussions on his Facebook page.

You can do the same thing with consumer-oriented companies, products, and brands. You can choose to "like" Starbucks coffee, Ludwig drums, Ford cars, or you name it. This puts you on the list for all sorts of promotional status updates fed to your News Feed, which can be either informative or highly annoying, depending on what's sent your way and how interested in it you are.

In essence, then, Facebook lets you become a fan of the entertainers, celebrities, and companies you like. You do this by liking an entity's Facebook Page—which is its home on the Facebook site.

Understanding Pages

Individuals on Facebook are represented by their Profile pages; other users become "friends" with a person to receive her status updates.

Businesses, celebrities, and public figures, however, aren't really "individuals" in the Facebook universe and as such don't have individual Profile pages or friends. Instead, high-profile Facebook users can create special Facebook Pages that serve as their public profiles on the popular social networking site.

What Is a Facebook Page?

What Facebook currently calls a Page (what it used to call a "fan page") is essentially a Profile page for very popular users. It's much like a regular Profile page but optimized for communication with large numbers of viewers.

With a normal Facebook Profile page for individuals, you try to get people to be your "friends." With a Facebook Page (note the capital "P"), you get people to "like" the Page and thus become fans. People who like a particular Page can read all about the person or organization, contribute to hosted discussions, view photos and videos, and receive all manner of status updates.

Who can create a Facebook Page? Just about any public person or entity. You can create Facebook Pages for businesses, brands, and products; for musicians, actors, and other celebrities; for politicians, public servants, and other public figures; and for school classes, public organizations, special events, and social causes.

For example, McDonald's is a business that has a Facebook Page. It uses its Page, as shown in Figure 18.1, to announce special deals and upcoming events. Music legend Brian Wilson has a Facebook Page, as shown in Figure 18.2; he uses it to talk with his fans, announce new albums, and post music, photos, and videos. Politician Sarah Palin has a Facebook Page (with more than 3 million followers!), which she uses to post statements and notes, as well as solicit donations, as you can see in Figure 18.3. Movie reviewer Roger Ebert even has his own Facebook Page, as shown in Figure 18.4, where he posts random thoughts and links to his movie reviews.

Note

Facebook requires you to create a Page—as opposed to a personal Profile—if you have more than 5,000 friends. This encourages public figures and companies to go the Page route over a traditional Profile page.

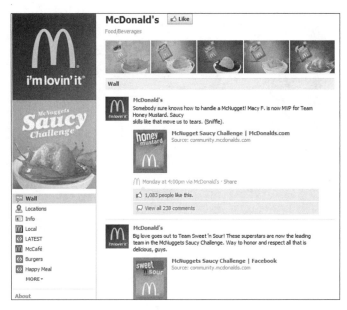

Figure 18.1. *McDonald's Facebook Page.*

Figure 18.2. *Brian Wilson's Facebook Page.*

Figure 18.3. *Sarah Palin's Facebook Page.*

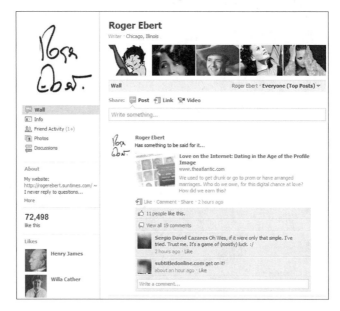

Figure 18.4. *Roger Ebert's Facebook Page.*

If you're a business or celebrity, a Facebook Page is a great way to keep in touch with your most loyal customers and fans. You can use your Page to announce new products and promotions, hold contests, and solicit customer opinions.

If you're a fan of a business or celebrity, a Facebook Page is a great way to connect with those you like to follow. You can find out the latest news and engage in interesting discussions with other fans.

Visiting a Facebook Page

So what do you find when you visit a person's or business's Page?

In many ways, a Facebook Page is like an online version of the traditional "fan club." They both function in much the same way, focusing on a particular person or organization, disseminating information from and about the topic at hand, and encouraging discussions among club/Page members. There are no in-person meetings, of course, but a Facebook Page is essentially your official contact to the person or organization at hand.

Finding a particular Page is as easy as searching for it. Just enter one or more keywords that describe the person or organization into the search box in the Facebook toolbar, and then click the Search button. When the search results page appears, as shown in Figure 18.5, click the Pages link in the sidebar; this will display all Pages that match your query. To view a specific Page, click the Page's name; to become a fan, click the Like button.

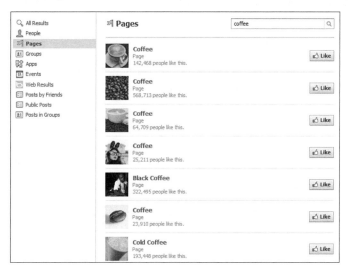

Figure 18.5. *Searching for Pages.*

That's right; you don't "friend" a Page as you would an individual on Facebook. Instead, you "like" it. It's pretty much the same thing, just different terminology—oh, and the page you like doesn't have to confirm your liking, as it would with a traditional friend request. When you like a Page, you essentially subscribe to it, so that all the status updates to that page appear in your News Feed on your Home page. Like I said, it's just like becoming a friend of that person or company, just without using the f-word.

As you might suspect, a "fan" Page is very similar to a standard Facebook personal Profile page. Facebook Pages have similar sections as do regular Profile pages, with a few extra features added. For example, a musician's Page might have an audio player for that performer's songs; some Pages include tabs for newsletters, promotions, discussion boards, and the like. Click the tab in the sidebar to view that tab's contents.

Creating Your Own Facebook Page

Any official representative of a business or organization can create a Facebook Page for that entity. If you're a celebrity or public figure, you can create a Page yourself or have a representative (such as your press agent) do it for you. Because a Page has to be official, competitors can't hijack your name and create a Page for you; nor can fans create "fan club" pages in your name.

Just as with most things Facebook-related, there's no charge to create a Facebook Page. The only thing you have to spend is your time.

Creating a New Page

Creating a Facebook Page is relatively easy. Follow these steps:

1. Go to www.facebook.com/pages/, and then click the Create Page button.

2. When the Create a Page screen appears, as shown in Figure 18.6, select the category for your Page:

   - Local Business or Place

   - Company, Organization, or Institution

   - Brand or Product

- Artist, Band, or Public Figure

- Entertainment

- Cause or Community

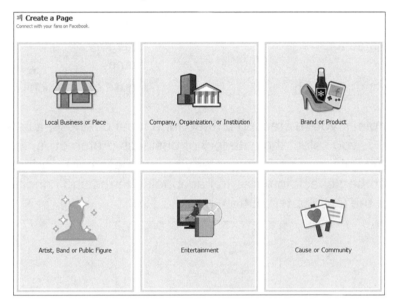

Figure 18.6. *Choosing the type of Page to create.*

3. Follow the instructions specific to the type of page you choose.

It gets a little tricky from here on out because the type of Page you choose to create determines additional options for the Page. Table 18.1 details the specific options available.

Table 18.1   Types of Facebook Pages

Type of Page	Options
Local Business or Place	Category Name of business or place Address/City/State/Zip Code Phone number
Company, Organization, or Institution	Category Company name

Type of Page	Options
Brand or Product	Category Brand or product name
Artist, Band, or Public Figure	Category Name
Entertainment	Category Name
Cause or Community	Cause or community name

For example, if you're creating a Page for a local business, as shown in Figure 18.7, you select the category of business (Automotive, Bar, Hotel, Restaurant/Café, and so forth); enter your business name, address, and phone number; check to agree to Facebook's terms and conditions; and then click the Get Started button.

Figure 18.7. *Creating a Local Business Page.*

Customizing Your Page

You're not done yet, however. You can now customize the look and feel of your Page, as well as which elements appear on the Page. You do this from the Get Started page that appears when you click the Get Started button, as shown in Figure 18.8.

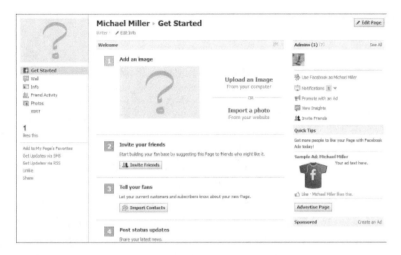

Figure 18.8. *Getting started with your new Facebook Page.*

Here's what you can do from the Get Started page:

- **Add an image.** This image appears at the top of the sidebar on your Page. This can be a picture of you, your product, or maybe your company or brand logo.

- **Invite your friends.** Invite people from your Facebook friends list to "like" your new Page.

- **Tell your fans.** Use this option to import names and addresses from an existing email contact list, and then invite them to become fans.

- **Post status updates.** Click the Post Update button to post your first status update.

- **Promote this Page on your website.** Click the Add Like Box to generate the HTML code to create a "Like" box for your Page that you can then add to your regular website or blog.

- **Set up your mobile phone.** This enables you to configure your Facebook account to receive status updates directly from your mobile phone.

Additional options are available when you click the Edit Page button on this page or on your Page. The resulting page has a number of different tabs that let you edit Page settings and add other elements to your page. Table 18.2 details the available options.

Table 18.2 Facebook Page Options

Tab	Options
Your Settings Email notifications	Posting preferences
Manage Permissions	Page visibility Country restrictions Age restrictions Wall tab shows (what appears on your Page's Wall) Default landing tab Posting ability (who can post what to your Wall) Moderation blocklist (list of terms to block in Wall posts) Profanity blocklist (enables you to block posts containing moderate or strong profanity) Delete page
Basic Information	Category Name Address Affiliation Birthday About Biography Awards Gender Personal information Personal interests Email Phone Website
Profile Picture	Use this tab to upload or change your Page picture.
Featured	Use this tab to add your own "likes" to the Page or to add profiles of featured owners of your Page.
Resources	Use this tab to promote your Page via advertising or invitations; add a Facebook Badge to your Page; or add a Like box to your website.

Tab	Options
Manage Admins	Use this tab to add or edit your Page's administrators.
Apps	Use this tab to add specific apps and elements to your page (more on this later in this chapter).
Mobile	Use this tab to register your mobile phone for uploading status updates, as well as download the Facebook iPhone app and sign up for Facebook text messaging.
Insights	Click this tab to see usage information for your Page.
Help	Access Facebook's Help system for Pages.

Selecting Page Elements

When you want to determine which elements appear on your Page, open the Edit Page page, and select the Apps tab. By default, Facebook includes the following elements:

- **Photos.** This is a tab for all the pictures you upload to your Page, either individually or in separate photo albums.

- **Links.** This tab lets you post links to web pages, blogs, photos, videos, and the like. You can even link to other Pages on Facebook.

- **Events.** This is a tab on your Page where you can post notice of upcoming events, appearances, and the like.

- **Notes.** This tab lets you post longer messages than you can via status updates. Think of your Notes page as a blog, a place to write to your heart's content.

- **Video.** This is a tab for all the videos you upload to your Page.

To delete any of these elements, open the Apps tab on the Edit Page page, and click the X next to the item to delete.

Facebook for Marketing

Facebook Pages, by their very nature, are promotional; they promote the person, group, or company behind the Page. That's understandable and a big reason why companies and public figures are creating Pages on Facebook.

Social network marketing—sometimes just called social marketing—is the latest big thing on the marketing front. Companies are flocking to Facebook, Twitter, and other social networking sites to promote their products and brands—and that might not be a bad thing for the rest of us.

One unique feature of social marketing is the way social networks like Facebook connect companies with their customers. Unlike most marketing, which consists of one-way communications (from the company to you), social media allows two-way communications, where comments from customers are as important as company pronouncements. This enables companies to form close bonds with their most avid or loyal customers—and for customers to feel like they're part of the brand's "family."

On Facebook, the prime source for this marketing activity is the company's Facebook Page. Companies can create pages for the company as a whole, for individual brands, or even for specific products. Another appealing facet of this is that creating a Facebook Page is free; the only cost to the company is the labor required to post and answer comments.

I could go on and on about how to use Facebook for marketing—and, in fact, I have. If you're at all interested in this, check out my book *The Ultimate Web Marketing Guide* (Que, 2010), available wherever fine books are sold. I devote a decent chunk of the book to social media marketing with a big focus on Facebook. If you're in business, it's something you need to pay attention to.

Chapter 19

Networking for Business—and for Jobs

As you know, Facebook is a great place to connect with family members and old friends. It's also a good place to connect with current and former coworkers, as well as others in your industry or profession. For that matter, many people use Facebook to help them look for new jobs; with all those "friends" you have on the Facebook site, at least one of them must know somebody somewhere who can help you get an in for a new position.

How, then, do you use Facebook on a more business-oriented basis? It's a matter of taking advantage of the appropriate Facebook features and of acting a bit more professional online.

Understanding Facebook Networks

Facebook is all about friends, which frequently means casual acquaintances. But you can also use Facebook to connect with others on a more professional basis—in particular, people who work at the same company you do.

What Facebook offers is a special type of group, called a *network*, devoted to a specific company—large companies, in particular. To join a company's network, you have to be an employee of that company, and you have to provide an active email address from that company. That's how you join the network, by the way—by entering your work email address.

Note that networks exist only for established businesses; there's either a network for your business, or there isn't. And if there isn't, you're out of luck, as Facebook doesn't let individuals create new networks.

That said, it's worth your while to see if Facebook has a network for the company you work for—especially if it's a big company with lots of offices in disparate locations. Let's face it: if you work in a five-person business, you don't really need a special Facebook group to connect with your coworkers. But if you work for an organization with thousands of employees across the nation or globe, connecting with your coworkers via Facebook could prove particularly useful.

What can you do in a work network? It's pretty much like any other Facebook group with membership limited to your work colleagues.

Note

Networks also exist for many schools and universities. Access to a school network is limited to current students, former students, and teachers who have a valid school email address. Because you probably graduated long ago and no longer have a school email address (if, in fact, you ever did), joining your old school network is probably out of the question. So we limit our discussion of networks to business networks only.

You can read status updates posted by company representatives, peruse company information, view photos of remote offices and work-related events, and join in lively discussions with colleagues near and far. It's a meeting place for the people you work with, plain and simple.

Joining Your Work Network

To join a company for your current employer, you must have a valid email address; this keeps non-employees and former employees from joining in the festivities. Assuming you have a work email address, follow these steps to join your company's network:

1. From the Facebook toolbar, click the down arrow and then select Account Settings.

2. From the Account Settings page, click the General tab.

3. Go to the Networks section and click the Edit link.

4. When this section expands, click the Join a Network link.

5. Enter the name of your company into the Network Name box, as shown in Figure 19.1. As you type, matching networks appear in a drop-down menu.

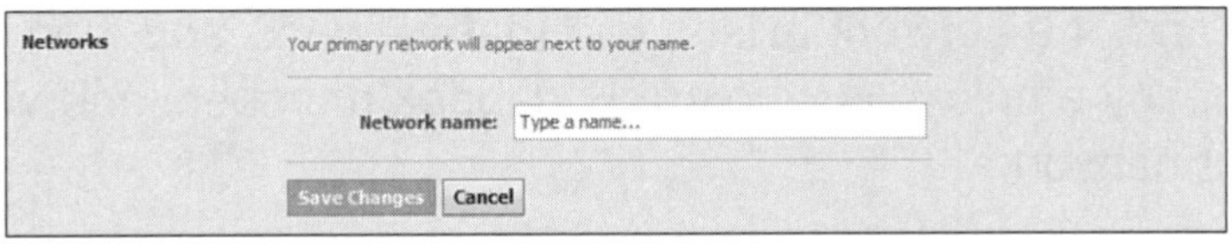

Networks	Your primary network will appear next to your name.
	Network name: [Type a name...]
	[Save Changes] [Cancel]

Figure 19.1. *Joining a work network.*

6. Select your company from the list.

7. Enter your work email address into the Work Email box.

8. Click the Save Changes button.

You should now receive a confirmation email at your work email address. Click the link in this email to finalize things. You now have access to your company's Facebook page, and everything that goes with it.

Networking Professionally

Although Facebook has its roots in personal social networking, it has also become a useful site for establishing professional connections. That's right; Facebook is more than just a site for friends and families. It's also a place to connect with coworkers, other professionals in your industry, and other business people in your city.

Finding Other Business Professionals on Facebook

There are many ways to find other business professionals (and potential employers) on the Facebook site. Let's look at a few.

One approach is to browse for friends of your business friends. Begin by identifying a colleague or business professional that is already in your friends list, and then go to that person's Profile page and browse her friends list. If you find someone with whom you would like to connect, invite that person to become your friend. Peruse that person's friends list to identify further potential business connections—and so on and so on. It's like a six-degrees-of-separation thing; eventually, you connect to people who can be of value.

Of course, if you're looking for connections within your company, the best bet is to join your company's network, as just discussed. Search for your company and, if a network exists, join that network. You then have access to all company employees who are Facebook members and who have joined that network.

You can also use Facebook's search function to search for relevant company names, industry buzzwords, and the like. Filter the search results by people, and you see a list of people who work for the company or in the industry in question. Invite these people to be your Facebook friends.

Managing Your Professional Contacts

After you've added a number of professional contacts to your Facebook friends list, it's good practice to create a group that consists of only these professional friends. You can then easily post status updates and send messages to this group of professional contacts.

Learn more about creating friends groups in Chapter 7, "Organizing Groups of Friends." Learn more about sending messages in Chapter 9, "Exchanging Private Messages."

Networking via Facebook Groups

Facebook hosts a large number of public groups focused on professional topics. These are groups devoted to a particular company, industry, or profession and tend to be where you find like-minded professionals on the Facebook site.

Use Facebook's search function to search for keywords related to your company, profession, or industry. When the search results page appears, filter the results by group. You can then join those groups that are most closely related to what you're looking for professionally.

Avoid making group posts that sound like advertisements or overt solicitations, especially solicitations for employment. You should offer genuine contributions, not self-promotion disguised as posts.

After you join a professional group, become an active participant. Participate in group discussions, respond to questions asked by other group members, and start your own conversations with others in the group. And when you post, be sure to provide useful and relevant information and advice to the group. Over time you become familiar with other group members, and you can invite them to join your friends list.

Job Hunting on Facebook

In addition to simple professional networking, you can also use Facebook to connect with prospective employers and seek out new jobs. To that end, Facebook is second only to LinkedIn for job hunters—and for employers seeking to fill new positions.

The key here is finding employers who use social networking sites such as Facebook to find prospective job applicants. Many companies look online to fill positions before paying for a job listing in a newspaper or on a job site such as Monster.com. The thinking is that it's better to fill the position for free than pay for the listing.

For that matter, you can often connect with potential employers before positions exist. You connect with someone on Facebook, make friends with them as it were, and he might think of you when something crops up in the future.

Reworking Your Profile

When you're in the job market, you need to present a professional face to potential employers. The first place to start is your Facebook Profile page, which can be reworked to function much like an online resume.

First, eliminate all unnecessary and potentially damaging personal information from your Profile. That means deleting information about your political and religious views, your favorite TV shows, likes and dislikes, and so on. Employers don't want or need to know that you're a fan of *I Dream of Jeanie*, follow Widespread Panic from concert to concert, and support the Libertarian party. That information seldom works in your favor and often works against you. Better to keep it short and sweet with the personal details.

Next, load up your Profile with all sorts of professional information, including employment history, professional accomplishments, and

Tip

You should also sort through your Facebook photos and delete those that present you in a non-professional matter. That includes some "recreational" photos; include too many golf photos and an employer might think you spend too much time on the links and not enough at the office.

the like. There are sections in your profile for much of this information; what doesn't fit naturally can be added to the Bio section in your Profile.

After you have your Profile cleaned up, make sure that it's set for public viewing. No sense going to all that work, and then hiding it from a future employer.

Becoming a Fan of Potential Employers

Facebook Pages are a great way to learn more about companies you want to work for. Not only can you find basic information about a company, you get first notice of company news and events.

To that end, you want to sign up for any potential company that has a Facebook Page. That means "liking" the company's Page, of course; after you do so, status updates from the company automatically appear in your News Feed.

Note

Learn more about Pages in Chapter 18, "Liking Public Pages."

Asking for a Job

Finally, let's not dismiss the simple act of using Facebook to tell people that you're looking for a job. You can do this by posting a status update to that effect—"Hey, I'm job hunting; anybody know of open positions?"

Of course, this probably isn't an option if you currently have a job and want to jump somewhere else. You don't want to tip off your current employer that you're looking, after all.

That said, this is a very direct way for the unemployed to make their interests known. Telling your Facebook friends that you're available sometimes turns up interesting work. Who knows which of your friends has knowledge of a decent job opportunity—or is looking to hire someone himself?

Keeping Your Personal and Professional Lives Separate

When you're using Facebook for professional purposes, you have to be careful about mixing your personal and professional lives. For example, you probably don't want to broadcast gossip (or even pictures!) about your drunken behavior at a weekend party to your boss or to potential employers. It makes sense to practice discretion about what you post in your status updates and to utilize Facebook's numerous privacy settings to limit what you display to whom online. (Friends lists are good for this.)

This goes beyond the obvious to the quite subtle. If you do a lot of spouting off about politics, religion, or other sensitive subjects in your Facebook status updates, some potential employers might think twice before giving you a hearing. For that matter, complaining about your current employer is sure to both get back to your boss (and nothing good comes of that) and cause potential employers to think you're either a whiner or a troublemaker, or possibly both. And nobody wants to deliberately hire someone like that.

To some degree, it comes down to the image conveyed by your Facebook presence. If you're less than discreet online, potential employers have to ask the question, "What kind of judgment does this person possess?" Poor judgment about what you say or post could carry over into what you do at work. In an employer's eyes, that would not be a good thing.

Speaking of images, know that your so-called friends on Facebook can work against you. Off-color remarks posted by a friend on your timeline are seen by others. If you're tagged in a questionable photo posted by a friend, that photo is going to show up in your stuff—and that includes photos from long ago and far away. A lot of people keep busy scanning old pictures and posting them on Facebook, tagging everyone included. You might not want these pictures made publicly available, but unless you can convince your friends to take them down, there you are.

And don't think that employers don't check you out on Facebook and other social networking sites. They most certainly do. You can't hide in plain sight; when you're an active job prospect, they're going to search for you and see what they find. If there's something up there that presents you in poor light, they'll find it.

Although you can try to hide some personal information by reconfiguring Facebook's privacy settings, there are ways around this. A large company might have someone on staff who went to the same school you did, and thus be able to view your information via the school network ties. Sometimes they deal in subterfuge, getting an intern to pose as a friend of a friend or whatever to get onto your friends list. In other words, if a company wants to see your stuff, they'll find a way.

So don't assume that your "private" information on Facebook will remain private. Instead, assume that a potential employer will look for and find everything posted by you and about you on Facebook. Take the effort to clean things up as much as you can—and refrain from mixing your personal and professional lives online.

Chapter 20

Finding Fun Games and Applications

Mafia Wars. *FarmVille*. LivingSocial. Family Tree.

You've seen them. Possibly you've played them or used them. Maybe you've even been annoyed by them—or rather, by posts about them from your friends. But what are they?

Mafia Wars, *FarmVille*, LivingSocial, and so on are Facebook applications. That is, they're games and little utility programs that run on the Facebook site. And they're very popular.

Understanding Facebook Applications

A Facebook application is simply a program or game that runs on the Facebook site. These applications are accessed from their own Facebook pages, and you use them while you're signed in to Facebook.

Now, these aren't big fancy applications like Microsoft Office or Quicken. No, they're small, typically single-purpose applications that are web-based in nature and add a bit of functionality to your Facebook experience.

Some applications build on the social networking nature of the Facebook site. Others are designed for more solitary use. Some are strictly functional. Others are more fun. The reality is that there are a wide range of these available; you're bound to find some that look interesting to you.

For example, the aforementioned Family Tree is designed to help you connect with other family members on Facebook. Goodreads helps you track, review, and publicize the books you're reading. The Causes application helps you mobilize your Facebook friends to support various charities and organizations. And you use the BranchOut app, as shown in Figure 20.1, to further your career networking and look for a job.

Note

Although some applications are developed by Facebook, most are created by third-party application developers. The vast majority of Facebook applications, including third-party apps, are available free of charge.

Figure 20.1. *Networking for a job with the BranchOut application.*

Then there are the apps that are a little less serious. Honesty Box is a quiz you can send to friends to find out what they really think about you. Which Marvel Superhero Are You?, as shown in Figure 20.2, is another quiz that determines whether you're more like Captain America or Spider-Man. The Pandora app lets you listen to and share music with your Facebook friends. And the Bumper Sticker app lets you create and post fun sayings to your Facebook page.

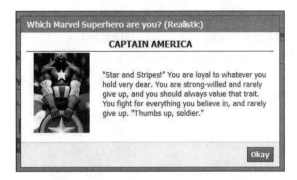

Figure 20.2. *Results from the Which Marvel Superhero Are You? application.*

Some Facebook applications are actually games—social games, to be exact. These are single-player or multi-player games that you play on the Facebook site, while you're logged in. *Mafia Wars*, *FarmVille*, and *Angry Birds* (as shown in Figure 20.3) are probably the most popular of these games, but there are a lot more than just these, some of which have millions of users. These games can be fairly addictive and become big time-wasters—which isn't necessarily a bad thing.

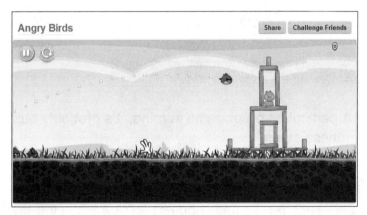

Figure 20.3. *The ever-popular Angry Birds game.*

Discovering Applications and Games

How do you find a Facebook application or game? You can either browse or search for apps; it's up to you.

If you're not sure what specific app or game you're looking for, you can browse apps by Most Recommended, Newest, and Friends Using—that is, those apps that your friends are using. All you have to do is visit the Facebook application directory, located at www.facebook.com/apps/. Figure 20.4 shows this directory.

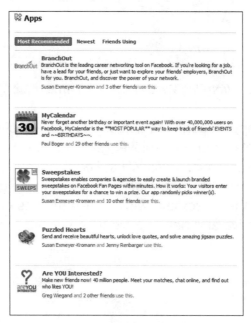

Figure 20.4. *Viewing the apps directory.*

If you have a particular app or game in mind, it's probably quicker to search for it. Follow these steps:

1. Enter the name of the app into the search box in the Facebook toolbar, and then click the Search button.

2. When the search results page appears, click Apps in the sidebar to display only applications in the search results.

3. Click the link for an application to display the Facebook page for that app.

Using an Application or Game

When you find an application you like, click the link for that application to go to that application's Facebook page. This page typically contains important information about that application—including, in many instances, reviews from users of that app.

If you want to use that application or play that game, follow the instructions to get started. You might be prompted with a Request for Permission to access your personal information on Facebook; you have to click the Allow button to proceed. (If you don't, you can't use the app or game.)

Viewing, Managing, and Deleting Your Applications

Want to see which applications you're using? There are probably a lot more than you might remember.

If all you want to do is see which apps and games you're using, go to the Apps section in the sidebar of your Facebook Home page, and then click More. This displays the Apps page, as shown in Figure 20.5, with all your apps listed. Click any link to view the page for that application.

Figure 20.5. *Viewing the applications you're using.*

If you want to edit the settings for a particular app, click the Pencil icon to the left of the app name, and click Edit Settings from the pop-up menu. You now see an Edit Settings dialog box for that application, like the one shown in Figure 20.6. Every app is different (some don't even have settings to edit!), so the contents of this dialog box differs from app to app. Make the desired changes, and then click the Close button.

Figure 20.6. *Editing settings for an application.*

To delete an application you're no longer using, click the Pencil icon and select Remove App. When you're prompted to confirm the deletion, click the Remove button.

Apps for Grown-Ups

Young people and older people use pretty much the same Facebook features, but they often use them in different ways. This is certainly the case with Facebook applications, where the apps used by the younger crowd tend to be much different than those used by those of us with a few more years under our belts.

Younger users, for example, tend to use a lot of the "quiz"-type applications, such as Honesty Box, IQ Test, and 21 Questions. They're also big on apps that purport to discover your true personality, deliver horoscopes and predictions, link together their Facebook friends, express moods and opinions, and send little virtual tchotchkes to each other. In other words, a lot of virtual time wasters.

Older users, however, tend to be a little less frivolous and bit more practical in their choice of apps. People our age like to use apps that help them connect to family members online, manage their schedules, track their favorite books and music, connect with business associates, and do things for our community. It's a different bag of apps than what your kids or grandkids use.

With that in mind, here are some of the apps I find most useful for or interesting to those of us of a certain age:

- **Birthday Calendar.** This app goes a few steps beyond Facebook's built-in birthday notifications, compiling all the birthdays of your friends and family members into a single calendar interface. It helps you plan ahead for upcoming birthdays, which is a good thing if you have a large family to deal with.

- **BranchOut.** A great app for those of us in the job market. BranchOut lets you post your resume, receive job alerts, and search for openings from within Facebook.

- **Causes.** This is a very popular application, designed to help publicize worthy causes and raise money for them.

- **Circle of Moms.** This is a social network within the Facebook network that lets moms connect with other moms to address the challenges of motherhood. This one has more than a million users.

- **Family Tree.** A great tool for finding your relatives—and staying in touch with them.

- **GoodReads.** This app helps you manage your book library, review books, and share your favorite books with your Facebook friends.

- **iLike.** Okay, this one's popular with the kiddos, too, but it's also a great app for us music-loving oldsters. iLike lets you share your favorite songs and playlists, as well as discover new music.

- **My LinkedIn Profile.** Great for job hunters or just those who want to connect with professional colleagues. This app adds your LinkedIn profile information to your Facebook Profile page.

- **MyCalendar.** An application that helps you keep track of friends' birthdays and Facebook events.

- **Pinterest.** An online "pin board" you can use to collect and share items of interest with your Facebook friends.

- **TripAdvisor.** Hotel and vacation reviews online.

- **TripAdvisor—Cities I've Visited.** A neat little app that creates an interactive travel map of places you've traveled, which you can then share with your Facebook friends.

- **Twitter.** If you're into the Twitter thing, this app enables you to follow your Facebook friends who also tweet and post your own tweets to Facebook.

- **We're Related.** A great app for finding far-flung relatives and building your family tree.

Then there are the games. Although I'd like to say that older, more mature users are less likely to play Facebook's social games, I don't think that's the case. I see too many posts about *FarmVille*, *Mafia Wars*, *Bejeweled Blitz*, and *Texas Hold'em Poker* to think otherwise. No, I'm pretty sure that a lot of old geezers waste as much time playing these games as do their more spritely offspring. It also appears that older users play many of the same games as do their younger counterparts.

Note

You can learn more about and start using any of these apps just by searching for them from the Facebook toolbar.

That said, I'm not going to go through a list of popular games here. You know what you like to play; you don't need me to tell you that. So feel free to search for what you like in the application directory. There are plenty of games to waste your time with there.

Blocking Annoying Games and Apps

Some people really like Facebook apps, especially playing games like *Mafia Wars* and *FarmVille*. I don't. I'm not a big game player, period. I especially don't care to hear about the games that my friends are playing. That's their business, and I don't want to be bothered.

The thing is I get bothered because many games and apps insist on posting status updates to my friends' feeds. Some apps post updates when a friend reads a new book or listens to a new CD. Some games post updates when a friend reaches a certain level or posts a certain

score (or, in the case of *Mafia Wars*, when they "off" someone important). These unwanted updates clog my News Feed and annoy the hell
out of me.

Fortunately, there's a way to block these app-generated updates from
your News Feed. Block an app or game once, and you never see an
update about that app again.

I talked about this trick back in Chapter 5, "Visiting Friends and Family
on Facebook," but it bears repeating here. To block an app or game
from posting status updates to your News Feed, you first have to find
one of these annoying posts. Point to the post to display the big X; this
displays a box underneath the post with three more buttons: Hide This
Post, Hide All by *Friend*, and Hide All by *Application*. (For example, if it's
a *FarmVille* post, the button reads Hide All by FarmVille.) Click Hide All
by *Application*, and Facebook blocks all future posts from this application or game from any of your friends.

Needless to say, I use this technique a lot. And I don't get too bothered by
unwanted application and game posts. Hurray!

Chapter 21

Buying and Selling in the Facebook Marketplace

Facebook is all about making social connections. But there's also a part of Facebook that is more about commerce than connections. The Facebook Marketplace, as it's called, is kind of like classified ads for and by Facebook members. You can use the Marketplace to find items for sale by your friends and others on Facebook or put stuff of your own up for sale.

Understanding the Facebook Marketplace

The Facebook Marketplace isn't a true marketplace, per se. It's really a database of classified advertisements. In this respect, it's more like Craigslist than it is eBay.

Like Craigslist, the Facebook Marketplace is a listing service for online classified ads. You don't actually purchase an item from the Facebook Marketplace; you contact a seller and arrange the purchase directly from him. Facebook doesn't get involved with payment, shipping, or anything like that.

The Facebook Marketplace is also like Craigslist in that there are no buyer or seller protections. If you send somebody money based on a Facebook ad and she doesn't ship the item, you're out of luck. Same thing if you sell something to someone and his check bounces. Don't even bother contacting Facebook about it.

It's all about personal transactions. You see an ad in the Facebook Marketplace, you contact the seller (via Facebook email), you agree on a purchase price, and you pay the seller directly. The seller then ships you the item, or if you live nearby, you go and pick it up. As I said, Facebook really isn't involved, saved for hosting the initial listing.

What can you buy or sell on the Facebook Marketplace? That's easy enough to see by examining the categories of goods and services listed on the Facebook site:

- **Stuff.** These are the "merchandise for sale" categories, including Baby & Kid Stuff; Books, Clothes & Accessories; Collectibles; Computers; Crafts & Hobbies; Electronics; Free; Furniture; Garage & Yard Sales; Health & Beauty; Home & Garden; Movies, Music & Video Games; Musical Instruments; Office & Biz; Sporting Goods & Bicycles; and Everything Else.

- **Vehicle.** That's right; you can find all manner of vehicles listed for sale in the Facebook Marketplace, including Airplanes, Boats, Cars, Commercial Trucks, Heavy Equipment, Motorcycles, Parts & Accessories, Power Sports, RVs, and Everything Else. (You can also shop by make of vehicle, in case you're specifically looking for a Ford, Honda, or whatever.)

- **Rentals.** The Facebook Marketplace isn't just for buyers and sellers; it's also for renters. The categories here include Apartments, Commercial, Condos, Garages, Homes, Open Houses, Roommates, Short Term, Storage, Vacations, and Other.

- **Real Estate.** If you're looking to buy or sell property, look here for Commercial, Condos, Farm/Ranch, Foreclosures, Homes, Land, Mobile Homes, Multi Family, Open Houses, Storage, Vacation Property, and Other.

- **Community.** This is similar to the "announcements" category in your local newspaper with news and announcements about all sorts of events.

- **Jobs.** Just like traditional classified ads, the Facebook Marketplace includes lots and lots of job listings that you can search by location.

- **Pets.** This is the category if you're looking to buy or sell dogs, cats, birds, fish, horses, and other animals.

- **Services.** It's not just about buying and selling things; the Facebook Marketplace is also a good place to buy and sell services, from music lessons to lawn care. Categories include Auto; Child & Elderly Care; Cleaning;

Coupons; Creative; Financial; Health & Beauty; Home, Legal; Lessons; Moving & Storage; Party & Entertain; Pet Services; Psychic; Real Estate; Tech Help; and Everything Else.

- **Tickets.** Want to buy tickets for a sold-out concert? Have some spare tickets to sell? Then this is the category for you.

Note

Even though it's very well integrated into the Facebook site, the Facebook Marketplace is actually a third-party application by Oodle, which is wholly endorsed by Facebook.

You can filter the items in these categories by location (X number of miles from your city or ZIP code) or just look at listings from your friends or friends of your friends. You can browse the categories or just search for something specific. And it's all done from within the main Facebook site.

Shopping for Something to Buy

The thinking behind the Facebook Marketplace is that buyers are more comfortable buying from people within or connected to their social circle. There's also the conceit, I suppose, that sellers who are Facebook members are somehow more reliable than sellers you find on other websites. I'm not sure I buy into that conceit, but do find that there's a lot of good stuff for sale on the Facebook Marketplace.

Browsing the Marketplace

When you're looking for something to buy, follow these steps:

1. Go to the apps.facebook.com/marketplace.

2. This opens the Facebook Marketplace page, as shown in Figure 21.1. By default, the page opens to listings in the city you specified in your Profile information. To change the city listed, click the Change link after the city name; when the Location dialog box appears, enter a new city name or ZIP code, and then pull down the Radius list and select how far away you want to search. Click the Submit button when done.

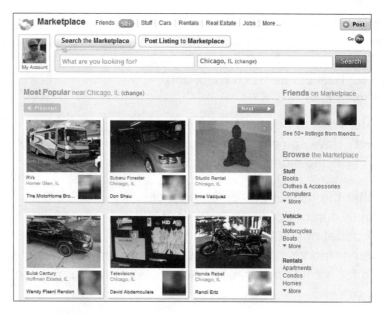

Figure 21.1. *The main Facebook Marketplace page.*

3. Click the tab at the top of the page for what you want to browse: Friends (items for sale by friends and their friends, that is), Stuff, Cars, Rentals, Real Estate, Jobs, or More. Alternatively, click a specific category in the right sidebar.

4. When the category page appears, like the one in Figure 21.2, click the subcategory you want to browse.

5. When the subcategory page appears, use the category-specific controls in the sidebar to further filter the results, if you want. For example, the Clothes & Accessories subcategory, as shown in Figure 21.3, lets you filter listings by type of item, price range, color, condition (new/used), or to only show those listings with photos.

6. To view a specific listing, click its title.

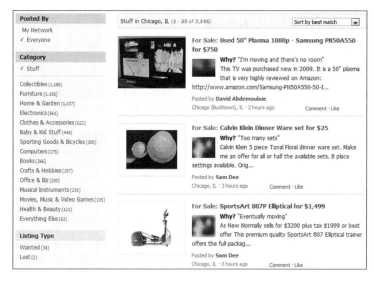

Figure 21.2. *A main category page.*

Figure 21.3. *A subcategory page with filters for price range and photos.*

Searching the Marketplace

If you have a specific item in mind, it's faster to search for it than to try to find it via browsing. Follow these steps:

1. From the Marketplace home page, click the tab for the category you want to search.

2. Enter a short description of what you're looking for into the Search box at the top of the page, as shown in Figure 21.4.

Figure 21.4. *Searching for items on the Facebook Marketplace.*

3. By default, Facebook searches within 50 miles of the city you specified in your Profile information. To change the search range, click the Change link in the Location box (next to the Search box). When the Location dialog box appears, enter a new city name or ZIP code, and then pull down the Radius list and select how far away you want to search. Click the Submit button when you're done.

4. To begin your search, click the Search button.

5. Facebook displays listings that match your query. To view a specific listing, click its title.

Viewing an Item Listing

Everything you need to know about an item for sale is on the item's listing page. This is the page you see when you click the item's title in the Marketplace listings. As you can see in Figure 21.5, the left column of the listing tells you about who's selling the item, while the item description fills up the right column. The item information includes details such as why the seller is selling it, a detailed item description, and photos of the item.

Tip

To learn more about the seller, which might or might not increase your confidence level, click the View My Profile link in the sidebar.

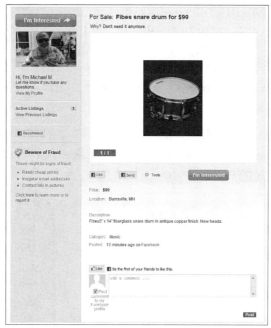

Figure 21.5. *A typical Facebook Marketplace listing.*

Sharing and Commenting on a Listing

If you think this item is something in which your Facebook friends might be interested, you can share it with them via a status update or private message. Click the Send button to display the sharing dialog box, as shown in Figure 21.6. Enter the name of a friend or group into the To: box, enter some accompanying text into the Message box, and then click the Send button to share the listing.

Figure 21.6. *Sharing a listing with friends.*

You can also comment on a given listing, just as you comment on a status update. Scroll to the bottom of the listing page, enter your comment into the Comments box, and then click the Post button. Your comment is posted at the bottom of the listing itself.

For that matter, you can "like" a listing just as you can "like" a status update. Just click the Like button below the item's picture to do just this.

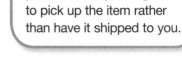

Tip

Given that Facebook, by default, displays only those listings within 50 miles of your location, you might want to pick up the item rather than have it shipped to you.

Contacting a Seller—and Buying Something

The Facebook Marketplace only facilitates the sales of merchandise; you don't involve Facebook in the actual sale. Instead, you contact the seller directly, haggle to your heart's content, and then pay the seller directly.

To contact a seller, follow these steps:

1. Open the item listing page and click the big green I'm Interested button.

2. When the New Message dialog box appears, as shown in Figure 21.7, enter a message to the seller into the Message box. This should be something along the lines of "I'm interested in buying this thing. Please contact me so we can discuss."

3. Click the Send button.

Caution

The usual cautions apply when you're purchasing any item through the Facebook Marketplace as they do when purchasing any item found via a classified advertisement. It's always good to see the item before you buy; you should take care when visiting a seller's residence; and after you get the item, it's pretty much *caveat emptor*— let the buyer beware.

Facebook sends your message to the seller. If the seller is interested, she gets back in touch with you via Facebook. It's up to the two of you to negotiate the final price, arrange payment, and get the thing shipped to you. In other words, it's now out of Facebook's hands.

Figure 21.7. *Responding to an item for sale.*

Selling Your Own Stuff

Where do the listings in the Facebook Marketplace come from? From your fellow Facebook members, of course. Which means that you can also use the Marketplace to list items you want to sell.

Listing an Item for Sale

There is no charge for listing items on the Facebook Marketplace. That's right, unlike eBay (but like Craigslist), all listings are free—the seller doesn't pay, nor does the buyer. So list as many items as you'd like; it doesn't cost you anything but your time.

To list an item for sale, follow these steps:

1. Go to the Marketplace home page, and click the Post Listing to Marketplace button.

2. When the Post a Listing dialog box appears, as shown in Figure 21.8, enter the name of what you're selling into the What Are You Listing? box.

3. Enter the selling price of the item into the Price box.

4. If your ZIP Code isn't correct, click the down arrow to change your location.

Figure 21.8. *Getting ready to list an item for sale.*

5. Pull down the Select a Category list and make a selection: Community, Houses, Jobs, Pets, Rentals, Services, Stuff (items for sale), Tickets, or Vehicle.

6. After you select a category, you are prompted to select a category-specific subcategory. Do so.

7. If prompted to select a second subcategory, do so.

8. Enter the reason for your sale into the Why Are You Listing It? box.

9. Enter a detailed description of the item into the Describe It box. Include all relevant details, including age, size, color, condition, and the like.

10. Because most items sell faster if they're accompanied by photos, you should take a few digital photos of what you're selling. To upload these photos, click Add a Photo to display the Open dialog box; navigate to and select the file(s) to upload, and then click the Open button.

11. Select the Post to Marketplace option. (Alternatively, you can opt to display this listing only to your friends by selecting the Post to My Friends Only option.)

12. Click the Post button.

The first time you post you are prompted for permission to share certain information; click the Allow button to do so. The item is now listed, and your listing is displayed.

Ending Your Listing

If and when a fellow Facebook member is interested in your item, you receive a message from that person, via Facebook, to that effect. You can then reply to that person and answer questions, accept the offer, arrange for shipment or pickup, or whatever. You are under no obligation to sell to any given person. What kind of payment you accept (cash, check, or whatever) is totally up to you.

After you sell an item, you need to remove it from the Facebook Marketplace. To do this, follow these steps:

1. Go to the Facebook Marketplace home page, and click the My Account link at the top of the page.

2. This displays the My Listings page, as shown in Figure 21.9, with the All Listings tab selected. Go to the listing you want to end and click the Manage link for that listing.

Figure 21.9. *All of your listings displayed on a single page.*

3. You now see the page for your listing. Go to the Manage This Listing section at the top of the page, as shown in Figure 21.10, and click the Close link.

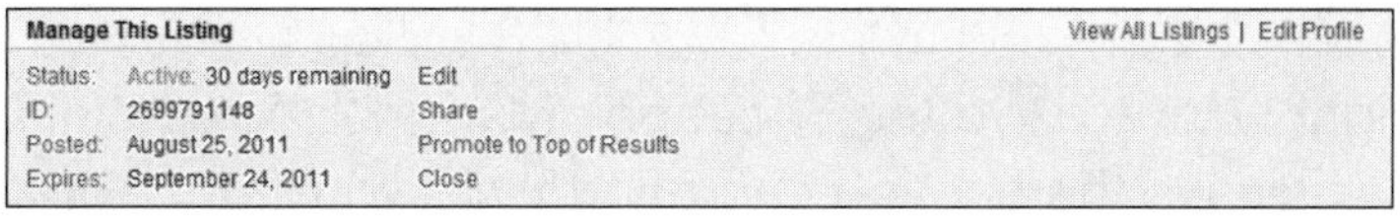

Figure 21.10. *Managing a listing.*

That's it; your listing is now closed.

Facebook Marketplace Versus eBay and Craigslist

If you've been around the Internet for any length of time, you're probably familiar with the other, more well-known marketplaces for buying and selling merchandise—eBay and Craigslist. You might be wondering how the Facebook Marketplace compares to both.

Comparing the Facebook Marketplace to eBay is a bit of an apples to oranges sort of proposition. That's because eBay functions as a full-service middleman. eBay not only facilitates item listings, it also handles all contact between buyers and sellers, offers payment services (via PayPal), provides assistance for shipping (via USPS and others), and offers a buyer protection plan to guard against fraudulent sellers. Facebook does none of these things.

In addition, eBay offers both fixed-price listings and those fun online auctions, where potential buyers bid up the price on items for sale. Facebook offers only fixed-price listings with no apparatus in place for conducting online auctions.

Craigslist offers a more relevant comparison. Like Craigslist, Facebook is essentially a service for online classified ads. Neither Facebook nor Craigslist offer payment services, shipping assistance, or buyer protection plans. Both are purely item listings only, leaving the ultimate sale for the buyers and sellers to arrange between themselves.

The big difference between Craigslist and the Facebook Marketplace is one of size. Craigslist offers many times more items for sale than does Facebook, so you're more likely to find what you want there. If you're a seller, Craigslist offers many more potential buyers than does the Facebook Marketplace; despite Facebook's size, relatively few members actually use the Facebook Marketplace.

So you might want to give the Facebook Marketplace a spin, but know that Craigslist is always there if you can't find what you want—or if you're selling and you don't get any buyers.

Chapter 22

Using Facebook on the Go

Most people connect with Facebook from their personal computers. But that isn't the only way to connect; you can also use your mobile phone to post status updates and read posts in your News Feed. Connecting in this fashion helps you keep in touch while you're on the go—or just waiting in line at the supermarket.

You can connect to Facebook from any mobile phone using simple text messages. But if you have a smartphone, like the Apple iPhone, you can use phone-specific Facebook applications to gain access to most of Facebook's features on the go. Even if all you have is basic Web access (no Facebook app), you can still connect to the Facebook site via your phone's web browser.

Connecting from Your iPhone

Because Apple's iPhone is the most popular smartphone on the market today, let's start by examining how you can connect to Facebook from your iPhone.

It all starts with the Facebook for iPhone application. You can find this app in the iPhone App Store; just search the store for "Facebook," and then download the app—it's free.

Viewing the News Feed

When you launch the Facebook app, you're taken immediately to the News Feed screen, shown in Figure 22.1. Like the News Feed on the main version of Facebook, this screen is divided into Top Stories and Recent Stories; scroll down the screen to view more posts. To update the News Feed, scroll to the top of the page and then pull the page down; you should see an Updating pane before the News Feed is refreshed.

Note

You can learn more about Facebook for the iPhone by going to the app's Facebook page at www.facebook.com/iphone/. The first time you launch the app, you need to enter your email address and password to log in to the Facebook site.

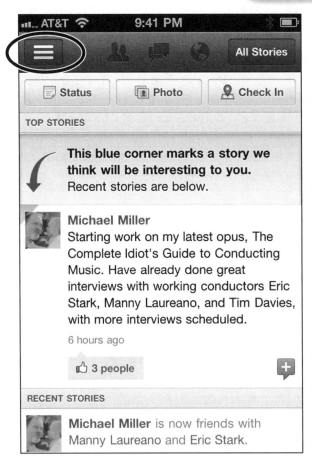

Figure 22.1. *The Facebook for iPhone News Feed.*

Each post in the mobile News Feed is similar to what you see on the web-based News Feed. You see the name of the poster, the post itself, and any photos or other attachments.

For each individual post, you can tap the poster's name to view that person's Facebook Profile page. If there are other links within the post, tapping a link opens the linked-to web page in a new screen.

Tip

To view a friend's Profile page from the News Feed, tap his name in a post.

If a post has a picture attached, tap the picture to view it full screen. If there's a video attached, tap the video to begin playback.

If a post has previous comments on it, you see a list of comments and likes beneath the body of the post. Tap this list to see who has liked the post or to read comments from others.

To comment on or "like" a particular post, tap the + next to the post and select Like or Comment from the balloon menu, as shown in Figure 22.2.

Figure 22.2. *Like or comment on a friend's status update.*

Press the Like button to like the post. To comment on the post, tap the Comment button to display the Comment screen. Enter the text of your comment into the large text box, and then click the Post button to post it.

By default, the News Feed page displays all your friends posts (it's the All Stories view), but it can also display other types of feeds. Tap the All Stories button at the top right of the News Feed page, and you see the scrolling selection menu, as shown in Figure 22.3. You can then choose to display the following choices:

Figure 22.3. *Changing what you see in your News Feed.*

- **All Stories.** This is the default view; it displays your Top Stories and Most Recent stories, just like your normal News Feed page.

- **Status Updates.** This displays only status updates (not photos or other notifications) from your friends.

- **Photos.** This displays the most recently uploaded photos from your friends.

- **Links.** This displays the most recent posts from your friends that include links to other web pages.

- **Pages.** This displays the most recent postings from those Facebook pages that you've liked.

- **Events**. This displays any upcoming events you have on Facebook.

- **Videos.** This displays the most recent videos uploaded from your Facebook friends.

Posting a Status Update

What I really like about using Facebook on my iPhone is being able to post status updates at any time, no matter where I am. Yeah, you have to hunt and peck with the iPhone's onscreen keyboard, but you get used to that.

To post a status update, follow these steps:

1. Go to the News Feed screen and tap the Status button at the top of the screen.

2. This displays the Update Status screen, as shown in Figure 22.4; use the onscreen keyboard to enter the text of your message.

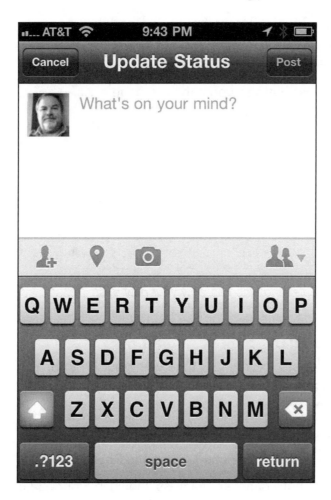

Figure 22.4. *Posting a new status update.*

3. To include a person you're with in your post, tap the With Who? button (the left-most button under the text box) and choose someone from your friends list.

4. To tag this update from a specific location, tap the Where Are You? button (second from the left under the text box) and select a nearby location.

5. To include a photo with this post, tap the Camera button and opt to either take a photo with your phone or upload a photo from your phone's photo library.

6. To determine who can view this post, tap the Privacy (globe) button to display the Audience panel, shown in Figure 22.5. From this list, select either Public, Friends, or a specific friends list.

7. Tap the Post button to post the message.

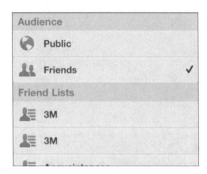

Figure 22.5. *Selecting who can view your new post.*

Posting a Picture

You can also post pictures you take with your iPhone. You can post either new pictures at the time you take them or photos you already have stored on your iPhone.

Follow these steps to take a new photo:

1. Go to the News Feed page and tap the Photo button.

2. When the photo panel appears, as shown in Figure 22.6, you have the option of taking a new photo (or video) or choosing an existing photo from your iPhone's photo library.

3. To take a new photo, tap the Take Photo or Video button; your iPhone now switches to camera mode, as shown in Figure 22.7. Snap a picture, preview the picture, and then tap the Use button.

4. To select a photo from your iPhone library, tap the Choose from Library button. You now see your iPhone's Photo Albums screen. Select an album, and then select a photo. When the next screen appears, as shown in Figure 22.8, click the Next button.

5. Whichever method you used, you now have the opportunity to add text to your photo post, as shown in Figure 22.9. Type whatever it is you want to say, and then click the Post button.

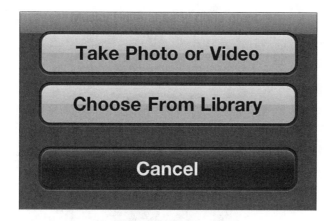

Figure 22.6. *Getting ready to post a picture.*

Figure 22.7. *Taking a picture with your iPhone.*

Figure 22.8. *Uploading a picture from your iPhone.*

Figure 22.9. *Adding text to a photo post.*

Checking In

Sometimes you just want to let your friends know where you are, without creating a major post about it. To "check in" to your current location, follow these steps:

1. Go to the News Feed page and tap the Check In button.

2. You now see the Where Are You? screen, shown in Figure 22.10. This screen lists places near your current location. Tap the place where you are, or enter a new place into the Search Places box.

3. You now have the opportunity to comment on your check-in. If you want to do this, enter your comments and then tap the Post button.

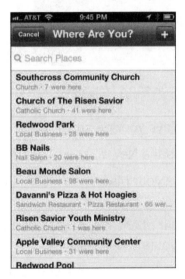

Figure 22.10. *Checking into a location.*

Navigating Other Functions

There's a lot you can do with the Facebook app—if you know where everything is. To access all the app's features, tap the Home button at the top-right of any screen. This slides the current screen to the right to display the Home screen, shown in Figure 22.11. From here you can tap any of the following:

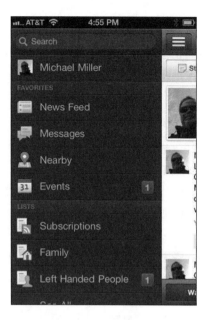

Figure 22.11. *The Facebook app's Home screen.*

- **<Your Name>.** Displays your personal profile page.

- **News Feed.** Displays the News Feed page that we've just discussed.

- **Messages.** Accesses your Messages inbox and displays your most recent private messages.

- **Nearby.** Displays a list of any of your Facebook friends who have checked into a location near yours.

- **Events.** Displays all Facebook events you're attending or have been invited to.

- **Lists.** Displays all your friends lists; tap a list to display a News Feed of posts from friends in that particular list.

- **Groups.** Displays all the Facebook groups you're subscribed to; tap a group to view the group's Facebook page and view posts in that group.

- **Apps.** Displays a variety of Facebook-created apps: Chat, Marketplace, Friends, Photos, and Notes; tap an app to use it. Tap See All to view other apps you're using.

- **Account.** Tap to view or edit your Facebook account settings and to log out of the Facebook app.

Viewing Friends' Profiles

Viewing a friend's Profile on your iPhone is relatively easy. Just tap the Home button to display the Home screen and then scroll to the Apps section and tap Friends. This displays a full list of your Facebook friends. When the friends list appears, tap a letter on the right side of the page to go to that alphabetical part of the list, or just scroll up or down the list. Scroll to and tap the name of the friend you want to view.

This displays your friend's Profile, like the one shown in Figure 22.12. There are three tabs at the bottom of the page: Wall, Info, and Photos. The Wall tab displays your friend's Wall, complete with recent status updates. The Info tab displays very basic (not complete) information about your friend. And the Photos tab displays your friend's photo albums.

Tip

To place a phone call to one of your friends, tap the telephone icon next to that person's name—if that person has publicly listed her phone number with Facebook, that is.

Figure 22.12. *Viewing a Profile page with Facebook for iPhone.*

When you're viewing a friend's photos, tap an album to view the contents; tap a picture thumbnail to view that photo full screen. After you've displayed one photo in an album, as shown in Figure 22.13, you can move to the next or previous photo by swiping the screen left or right. Return to the containing album by tapping the Done button at the top left of the screen.

Figure 22.13. *Viewing a friend's photo on your iPhone.*

You can post a message to your friend's Wall simply by tapping the Write Post button near the top of the page. Likewise, you can share a photo with your friend by tapping the Share Photo button.

Checking Messages

You can also use your iPhone to check your Facebook messages while you're on the go. If you have private messages from other users, they show up in your Facebook inbox. You access the inbox on your iPhone by tapping the Home button to go to the Home screen, and then tapping Messages.

To view messages from your friends, tap the Messages button at the bottom of the inbox screen. As you can see in Figure 22.14, messages are grouped by sender. To view all messages (including chats) from a given user, tap that person's name.

Figure 22.14. *Viewing messages in your inbox.*

The inbox also displays other information. To view notifications from pages you've liked, tap the Other button at the bottom of the inbox screen. To see which of your friends are currently online, tap the Online button.

Chatting with Friends

Why might you want to see who is online? So you can chat with them, of course. To that end, you can easily access Facebook's real-time text chat from your iPhone.

To access Facebook Chat, tap the Home button to display the Home screen, and then go to the Apps section and tap Chat. This displays a list of friends who are currently online. Those friends available for chat have a green dot next to their names; those who are "asleep" or otherwise unavailable have a crescent moon instead.

To initiate a chat session, tap that person's name. The chat screen now appears, as shown in Figure 22.15; use the onscreen keyboard to enter your initial message, and then tap the Send button. Your ongoing conversation displays in the top of the window.

Figure 22.15. *Chatting in real time with Facebook for iPhone.*

Connecting from Other Mobile Phones

The iPhone isn't the only smartphone or tablet supported by Facebook. There are Facebook apps for all the following devices:

- Android
- Blackberry
- INQ
- Nokia
- Palm
- Sidekick
- Sony Ericsson
- Windows Mobile

All these apps work similarly to the Facebook for iPhone app.

If your web-enabled phone doesn't have a dedicated Facebook app, you can still use your phone's web browser to connect to the Facebook Mobile website. Just navigate to m.facebook.com and you see a version of the Facebook site that's optimized for mobile browsers. In fact, the mobile site looks almost identical to the Facebook mobile app; the first page is the News Feed, and from there you can tap the Home button to display the Home screen and other features.

Connecting via Text Message

How can you connect to Facebook if you don't have a fancy smartphone? It's easy, really, as Facebook enables you to post via simple SMS text messages from any mobile phone. You can also receive text messages when your friends post to their Walls.

To use Facebook via text, you first have to activate your individual phone. Here's how to do it:

1. Click the down arrow on the Facebook toolbar, and then click Account Settings.

2. When the Account Settings page appears, click the Mobile tab.

3. When the Mobile tab appears, click the Add a Phone button.

4. When the Add Mobile Phone dialog box appears, enter your Facebook password and click Confirm.

5. You now see the Activate Facebook Texts dialog box, as shown in Figure 22.16. Select your country and mobile phone carrier from the lists, and then click Next.

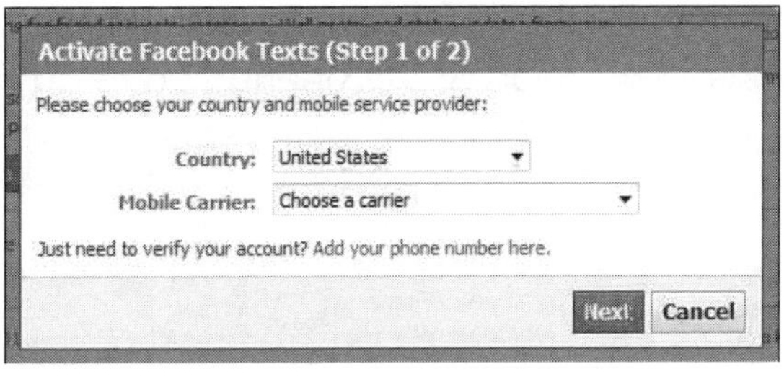

Figure 22.16. *Activating Facebook texts.*

6. The Step 2 dialog box contains instructions on how to register your phone. You need to use your phone to text the short message displayed here (typically just the letter "F") to the number listed (32665 or FBOOK), and then click Next.

7. Facebook replies to your text with a unique mobile activation code. Enter this code into the Step 2 dialog box on your computer screen.

8. If you want your friends to see your mobile phone number, check the Share My Phone Number with My Friends box. If you want to keep your number private, uncheck this box.

9. Click the Next button.

10. Facebook displays the Mobile Settings page shown in Figure 22.17. This page lists the various mobile settings that affect your Facebook use. Click the Edit link next to any setting to reconfigure it.

Figure 22.17. *Configuring text messaging for your Facebook account.*

After you have your phone activated and configured, you can send status updates to Facebook via text messages from your phone. All you have to do is send your texts to 32665 (or FBOOK), and you're good to go.

Facebook Mobile for Old Farts

Here's a good question: Do us older folks use our phones as much as our kids do? I think not—although that could be changing.

As you're well aware, the young people today are born with mobile phones grafted onto their palms. They emerge from the womb texting about the experience: "dr hit me rdy 4 lnch."

To the younger generation, texting is as natural as breathing. It's no surprise that they often opt to do the Facebook thing via cell phone, too. They always have their phones with them—their computers, not so much. So they do the configuration thing, receive friend's updates and messages via text messages, and make their own posts via texts. It works well for them.

We older folks, however, are less comfortable with and often less skilled at the whole texting thing. My stepdaughter can do 10 texts in the time it takes me to peck out a single one, and I've yet to figure out all the shortcuts and abbreviations she uses. It's kind of like a foreign language to me, one that requires the punching of teeny buttons with pudgy fingers. It's not a good fit.

So my sense is that grown-ups use Facebook on their phones far less often than do their offspring. That doesn't mean it doesn't have its place in your bag of tricks or that you'll never do it. But I'm guessing you'll use your phone to read more posts than you make, while younger folks do a lot of both reading and posting from their phones.

Now, that might be changing, especially as parents discover that texting could be the only way to communicate with their young ones. And if it does change, then you'll probably be doing a bit more posting to Facebook from your phone, too. But in general, our generation isn't as focused on the "now" as is the younger generation; more often than not, we can wait to do our social networking when we're back at the computer, thank you very much.

Chapter 23

Exploring Twitter, LinkedIn, and Other Social Networks

Facebook wasn't the first social network, and it won't be the last. There are lots of other social media out there competing for your attention, and you might be tempted to use one or more of them—either in place of or in addition to Facebook.

What other social networks exist today—and how do they compare to Facebook? Read on to learn the answers to these and other weighty questions.

Examining Other Social Networks

With 750 million users, Facebook is the king of social networks. But it's not the only social network in use today; there are some strong competitors that you might want to check out.

Why might you want to branch out beyond Facebook—or even leave Facebook for another network? There might be a number of reasons. Maybe another social network better serves your personal or professional needs. Maybe you just like how another network works better than Facebook. Or maybe all your friends or colleagues are using another network instead of Facebook. Whatever the reason, there are some interesting social networks to consider.

Google+

The newest competitor in the social networking game comes from Google. It's called Google+, and it aims to do pretty much everything Facebook does, except a little different—and, perhaps, a little better.

Google+ launched in June 2011; within its first few weeks of operation (invitation-only, by the way), it had attracted more than 20 million users. That makes Google+ one of the fastest-growing services on the Internet and an instant competitor to Facebook.

Looking at Google+ (plus.google.com), you can see that it offers pretty much the same set of features you find on Facebook. Both Google+ and Facebook offer text-based status updates, photo and video sharing, instant messaging/chat, and versions for mobile phones. All the basic stuff is there.

What's different is how Google+ does things. As you can see in Figure 23.1, the Google+ interface is a lot less cluttered than what you're used to with Facebook. Google+ is also a bit more organized than Facebook's somewhat-chaotic way of doing things, especially in the way it lets you organize friends into small groups, called *circles* (as in "circles of friends"). You can easily assign a friend to one or more circles, and then post status updates only to selected circles.

Note

Learn more about Google+ in my upcoming book, *The Complete Idiot's Guide to Google+* (Alpha Books, 2011).

Figure 23.1. *The Google+ social network.*

There are some other minor differences, but Google+ is meant to be a head-to-head competitor to Facebook. Not surprisingly, Google+ has generated a lot of attention, especially among early adopters, tech experts, and some of the younger generation. That said, none of my older friends have tried it out yet. That probably says something.

LinkedIn

LinkedIn (www.linkedin.com) is a different kind of social network. Oh, it offers many of the same features and functions as Facebook, but as you can see in Figure 23.2, it's positioned as a business-oriented social networking site. The site currently has more than 120 million registered users with an additional 1 million people joining each month.

Figure 23.2. *LinkedIn, the social network for business professionals.*

True to its targeting as a business-oriented network, LinkedIn is used primarily by business professionals. The average age of a LinkedIn user is 41; the average annual income is $109,000. Fully 64% of LinkedIn users are male, and 80% are college graduates. Most are successful in their chosen professions, with 46% describing themselves as "decision makers" in their companies.

Unlike Facebook, which most people use primarily to keep in touch with friends and family, people use LinkedIn to expand their list of business contacts, to communicate with colleagues within their industry, and to keep abreast of developments in their profession. You can network with your

LinkedIn contacts to find employment, make a sale, or explore business opportunities.

As such, LinkedIn is used by many professionals to supplement Facebook, not to replace it. If you're in the job market or just want to expand your industry connections, it might be worth giving it a spin.

MySpace

Before Facebook hit the jackpot, MySpace (www.myspace.com) used to be the number-one social network. That was several years ago, and although MySpace is still popular, it's fallen on hard times.

Originally, MySpace had a similar user base as Facebook, focusing primarily on college students. Over the years, older users gravitated away from MySpace to Facebook, leaving MySpace with a slightly younger demographic—junior high and high school students, primarily.

In recent years, however, MySpace has become known as a site for musicians, actors, comedians, and other entertainers, as well as their fans. As you can see in Figure 23.3, the site's focus on music and entertainment is all too apparent; it's less a social networking site than one for younger music and movie lovers.

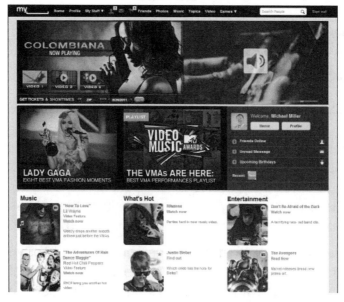

Figure 23.3. *MySpace, a social network for music and movie lovers.*

I can't say I'd recommend anyone reading this book to drop Facebook in favor of MySpace. That said, if you're a music lover, you might check to see if your favorite artists are on MySpace—and if so, you can follow them there.

Twitter

Then there's Twitter (www.twitter.com). As you can see in Figure 23.4, Twitter is less a social network than it is a broadcast service for short text messages. (Technically, it's a form of social media known as *microblogging*.) You don't really connect with others via Twitter; instead, you sign up to "follow" people you like, and then read all the posts they make.

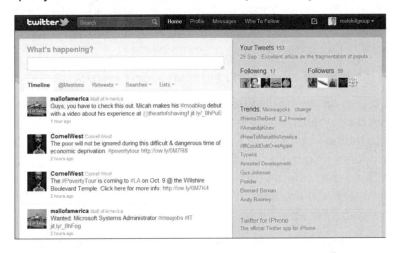

Figure 23.4. *Twitter, a place to follow what interesting people are tweeting.*

Twitter works much differently than does Facebook. Users post short text messages, called *tweets*, from their computers or mobile phones. These tweets (limited to 140 characters) are displayed to a user's followers and are searchable via the Twitter site.

Although Twitter isn't a full-featured social network like Facebook, it is quite popular, with more than 200 million users. That said, the vast majority of Twitterers are followers and never tweet—which shows you how different it is from Facebook.

I know a lot of folks who belong to both Facebook and Twitter. They use Facebook to connect with friends and family, and Twitter to follow a few high-profile celebrities or news organizations. That's fine; it's difficult to see Twitter replacing the social interactions that make Facebook so popular.

Using Third-Party Tools to Consolidate Multiple Social Networks

If you fancy yourself a multiple social network kind of person, get ready to geometrically increase the amount of time you spend networking online. Unless, that is, you use a tool that lets you create a single update and post it to multiple social networking sites—and consolidates all the posts from all your friends on all those sites in a single place.

What are the best of these consolidation tools? Here's a short list:

- **HootSuite (www.hootsuite.com).** This one is a self-described "social media dashboard" designed more for businesses than individuals. In addition to letting you post to Facebook, Twitter, LinkedIn, and other social networks, it also lets you track when you're mentioned on those sites. HootSuite also offers various team collaboration features, including task assignment and tracking. It's really full featured, but probably overkill for the average Facebooker.

- **Ping.fm (www.ping.fm).** A one-stop posting service that posts your messages to Facebook, Twitter, MySpace, LinkedIn, and other social media—including WordPress and Blogger blogs, if you have them. It does not, however, let you read posts from multiple networks; it's a posting-only service.

- **Seesmic (www.seesmic.com).** A tool that consolidates posting and reading posts from Facebook, Twitter, LinkedIn, and other social media. It's available in desktop software, mobile, and web-based versions, although it tends to target heavy business users rather than individuals.

- **TweetDeck (www.tweetdeck.com).** This is my personal favorite social media consolidation program. TweetDeck lets you both make and monitor posts to and from Facebook, Twitter, LinkedIn, MySpace, and other social media. It's free and easy to use, and even has a nice mobile app for reading and posting while on the go.

Which of these tools should you use? Well, unless you're a heavy user of more than one social network, I'd say none of the above; you don't need to. That said, if you're posting multiple times a day on two or more social networks and trying to keep track of friends across those same networks, take a look at TweetDeck. It's free and does what you need it to do with a minimum of fuss and muss. The other alternatives are also good, but might offer either a little less or a lot more than you really need.

Note

Learn more about TweetDeck in my companion book, *Sams Teach Yourself TweetDeck in 10 Minutes* (Sams Publishing, 2010). It's available in Kindle format from Amazon.com or in other electronic book formats from www.quepublishing.com.

Do You Really Want to Leave Facebook?

Okay, so there are other social networks out there. But should you be thinking about leaving Facebook and taking up with one of them?

In general, I'd say no—especially for us older users.

As attractive as another social network might or might not be, what makes Facebook such a good thing is its sheer size; with more than 750 million users, just about everyone you'd want to communicate with is there. The largest competitors have fewer than one-third as many users, which means you're less likely to find friends and family there—and sharing with friends is what social networking is all about. Why bother joining a different social network if no one's there to share with?

Then there's the issue of actually picking up and leaving Facebook. Let's face it; after you get started with Facebook, you have a lot invested there. You've made dozens or hundreds of friends, uploaded all your digital photos, and essentially made a home for yourself there. Because of all the connections you've established, Facebook becomes exceedingly difficult to leave. Can you imagine abandoning everything you have on Facebook and starting fresh on another site? I can't.

So it's all about where your friends are and where your stuff is—which, for most of us, is Facebook. It really doesn't matter if another site does the social networking thing a little better or different; Facebook is where we live and where we'll stay.

That doesn't mean, however, that you can't also play in another backyard. A lot of folks our age maintain both Facebook and LinkedIn accounts, for example, because of the business networking that the latter offers. Other folks do Facebook and the Twitter thing because they like to follow big-name stars or whatever. There's nothing wrong with that. They're not abandoning Facebook; they're just adding to their networking possibilities.

Chapter 24

Connecting Facebook to Other Sites and Services

Did you know that you can make posts to your Facebook feed from other websites? That's right, Facebook makes it easy to share things you find interesting, such as news stories or blog posts, without having to copy and paste web page addresses and the like.

For that matter, some websites are *so* connected to Facebook that they report everything you do to your timeline and ticker. Songs you've listened to on Spotify, stories you've read on Yahoo! News—it's all part of one big social connection, hosted by Facebook.

Liking and Sharing Pages

Find something interesting on the Web that you'd like to share with your Facebook friends? It's easy enough to do by simply "liking" the page.

When you're visiting another website or blog, look for the Facebook button. This might be a simple Facebook logo in some sort of "sharing" section or a more clear-cut Facebook Like, Facebook Recommend, or Share on Facebook button, like the one shown in Figure 24.1. Click this button to share the item you're reading.

Figure 24.1. *Look for the Facebook button*

Often you are prompted to add a comment about the item. This might be in the form of a pop-up comments box, like the one in Figure 24.2, or in a separate Facebook window, like the one in Figure 24.3. (You might also be prompted to supply your Facebook login information, if you haven't yet linked this site to your Facebook account.) Enter your comment and click the Share Link or Post to Facebook button to post a link to this item as a status update on Facebook, as shown in Figure 24.4.

Figure 24.2. *Commenting on a shared article.*

Figure 24.3. *Another prompt to comment on a shared article.*

Figure 24.4. *An article shared in your Facebook feed.*

Connecting Other Sites to Facebook

Here's one I'm sure you've encountered. You go to register with another website, and you're given the option of signing in with your Facebook ID. This process is a convenience; instead of creating user accounts for each and every site you visit, you use a single account (Facebook) to log into multiple sites.

What's the benefit of signing in to a site with your Facebook ID? Fewer IDs and passwords to remember, obviously. In addition, if you choose to "like" or share a page, that site already knows your Facebook ID, so it can post that recommendation to Facebook without first asking for your username and password.

Now, most sites that let you sign in this way don't feed your activity back to Facebook—but that's changing. In fact, Facebook is encouraging sites to use its Open Graph technology to tightly connect what you do on those sites to your Facebook account. The result is that all your activities on that site get reported back to Facebook, and often end up posted as items in your friends' tickers.

Instead of hoping that you'll manually "like" or share a page or story to Facebook, you're asked once—just once—if you want to connect a given site to your Facebook account. From that point on, everything you do on that site gets fed back to Facebook. You're not asked to approve each activity as it occurs, your permission is now implicit.

Your activities on these connected sites are automatically fed to the ticker that appears on your and your friends' Home pages; they also appear on your Profile page's timeline. They typically don't appear in any News Feeds, however, unless Facebook for some reason deems something an important event. (Don't ask me how it does this; it doesn't tell anybody.)

What kinds of sites connect to Facebook in this fashion? News sites, media sites (Netflix, Hulu, and so on), lifestyle sites, games, you name it. Pretty much any site you can visit can connect to Facebook via Open Graph.

Note

Spotify (www.spotify.com) is a popular online streaming music service.

Let's look at an example. I recently connected my Spotify account to Facebook. Now every song I listen to on Spotify is now reported in my ticker, and a Spotify item appears on my Profile page, as shown in Figure 24.5. I don't get asked if I want each song reported, it just happens. (And if a Facebook friend is using Spotify, he can play those same songs directly from his Facebook page.)

Figure 24.5. *Music listened to on Spotify reported on the Facebook timeline.*

Similarly, I've also connected Yahoo! News to Facebook. Every news story I read (or to be more exact, visit; technology isn't smart enough yet to know if I actually read the thing) is reported back to Facebook, no questions asked. These stories appear one by one in my ticker, and in a Yahoo! News section of my Profile page, as shown in Figure 24.6. If a Facebook friend wants to read one of these stories, all she has to do is click it.

Figure 24.6. *Yahoo! News stories read reported on the Facebook timeline.*

These are just two examples of "social plug-ins," as Facebook calls them. If you want to make all your activity on a given site visible on Facebook, answer in the affirmative when you're prompted on that site. If you'd rather keep your activity private, click No instead.

To Connect, or Not to Connect—That Is the Question

All your online activities, across multiple sites, connected into a single stream. Sounds kind of cool, doesn't it?

Facebook's intent with Open Graph is to help you share everything you do online—via the Facebook site, of course. This creates a larger web of connections, tracking your activity across the entire Internet.

It's certainly a great way to share your online activities with your Facebook friends. You find a news story you like, you share it with your friends, no buttons to click. You listen to a great song online, you share it.

The problem is, what if you read a news story you don't want to share? Or you start reading and discover you don't really like that story at all? What if you listen to a song you'd be embarrassed to have your friends know you're listening to, or play a game that you shouldn't be playing? When you give a site permission to connect your activity to Facebook, it connects *all* your activities, even those you might have second thoughts about.

Some people—well, lots of folks at Facebook, anyway—are really hyped on this new Open Graph connect everybody to everything initiative. Other people are less thrilled. It's fair to say that some folks are downright up in arms about the privacy implications of Facebook knowing everything you do on all kinds of sites across the Web. It's a lot of information and power centralized in one place.

I'm not that fond of it all for the simple reason that I really don't want to share that much about what I'm doing online. Look—my friends and family don't need to know that I'm listening to ABBA this morning, or just got done reading a story about Scarlett Johansson's latest nude pictures. Not that I'd be embarrassed about either one (well, maybe not), but rather I don't feel that every little track I make across the Web is interesting enough to post publicly.

I know that's Facebook's intent—to create a massive public social web—for no other reason but it profits from it. After all, the more Facebook knows about you and what you do, the more and more targeted advertising it can sell. But that's not something I necessarily want to participate in; Facebook isn't paying me for sharing that information, after all.

So I choose to opt out of this whole sharing from other sites thing. I'll post to Facebook what I want people to know, and nothing more. I'd like to keep a little of my private life private, if you don't mind.

Getting the Most Out of Facebook—for Grown-Ups

I've spent this entire book showing you how to use Facebook with a particular emphasis on those features and approaches of interest to a slightly older audience—grown-ups, for want of a better word. But I'd like to wrap things up by talking about how Facebook works for grown-ups in the real world, like what you can expect to find when you go online and start getting all friendly like.

When you first sign up for Facebook, your first group of friends will likely be those people with whom you communicate on a fairly regular basis already. I'm talking coworkers, family members, close friends—anybody who's in in your email contact list. It's easy for Facebook to identify these folks and hook you up, so these are your first Facebook friends. Although talking to these people on Facebook is unique for a little while, it really doesn't offer a huge improvement over how you're already communicating.

Next up, you'll probably track down and "friend" other family members. Expect to add brothers and sisters, aunts and uncles, nephews and nieces, and children and grandchildren to your friends list. In this instance, Facebook ends up being a fairly convenient way to broadcast family information without having to write a lot of individual emails or make a lot of phone calls. If you need to report the latest medical emergency, work promotion, or school accomplishment, just post a single status update and the entire family is notified. Easy as pie.

The influx of family members should then inspire you to post a raft of family photos to the Facebook site. Thus inspired, prepare to set aside an evening or two to organize your digital photos and upload them to Facebook. You might even want to upload some home movies, if you have them in a handy digital format. Your family will appreciate the effort.

Of course, while we're thinking about photos, you'll also be looking at the photos that your family members have uploaded. Chances are you haven't seen most of them, so you can spend some time catching up with your relative's activities, visually.

Those of us in the working world soon add our business associates to the list. I'm talking current and past coworkers, people we work with in other companies, folks we meet at business seminars and conventions, and even other local businesspeople we know. Facebook is quite useful for keeping in touch with other professionals with whom we might not otherwise have regular contact. Just remember to keep things fairly professional when you're dealing with this group of friends.

For many adult users, the next logical step is to add your neighbors to your Facebook friends list. This takes a bit more effort, as you actually have to know your neighbors' names (I don't, sorry to say), and then search for them on Facebook. While you're at it, don't forget to add those former neighbors with whom you've always meant to keep in touch, but haven't; they'll appreciate it.

Finally, you're going to start getting curious about your *old* friends. I don't mean those people older than you, but those guys and gals you hung out with in your youth. I'm talking high school buddies, college pals, and the like.

Now, tracking down old friends on Facebook is a bit of a challenge. You can search by name, of course, but good luck finding that one John Brown you used to hang with among the thousands of similarly named Johns on the Facebook site—especially as your Mr. Brown might be living in a different part of the country now.

It's even worse trying to find women who've gotten married and divorced and married again (repeat as necessary). I'm sure you have no idea that the Sally Jones you went to school with in Chicago is now Sally McWhorter of Portland, Oregon.

What you have to do find these folks is just keep plugging away. Search and search and search some more, and don't forget to look on your friends' friends lists; it's possible that one of your friends has already found this person and done the connection thing.

You should also be prepared to receive a lot of friend requests from people you know, people you think you might know, and people who you either don't remember or never heard of. That's part of participating in the Facebook community. Accept as many requests as you want, but pay particular attention to those who don't necessarily ring a bell; they might be some of your long-lost schoolmates that found you before you found them.

It's also possible that they're people you went to school with but weren't necessarily close to. I can't tell you how many Facebook "friends" I have who know me from high school even though I barely, if at all, remember them. But that's okay; there's no harm connecting with these folks in the virtual manner, at least that I can tell.

When you do connect with old friends, be prepared for some major shocks; there's been a lot of stuff happening since you've last seen them. People get married, get divorced, move, change jobs, have kids, or even change sexual persuasions. I admit to being a little surprised at the handful of formerly straight friends who now say they're gay, and for some I thought were gay who are now straight. I'm equally surprised to find the occasional minister or priest on my old friends list. (None of us were priests back then, I can tell you.)

You might also be surprised—and a little shocked—to see what your old friends look like these days. I admit that I've aged, there's no denying that, but some of my friends…well, the years have not been kind. It's interesting to try to connect the dots between what someone looked like in high school and what they look like today, but I swear, some of these odd-looking ducks are strangers just claiming to be the same people I used to know. There's no resemblance there that I can see.

You also need to be prepared by what your old friends are doing and saying and thinking. When you hang out with a bunch of kids in high school, you all tend to think and act alike. What a shock, then, to find old friends who have become ultra-conservative right-wingers, tree-hugging environmentalists, religious cultists, free love swingers, or whatever. You might think you knew them then, but they're not necessarily the same people today. Life does that to you.

In fact, I guess that's the true lesson we learn from connecting with friends and family on Facebook: Life goes on. And Facebook, fortunately, helps us catch up and stay caught up with the lives of everyone we know. That's what I like about Facebook and why I use it every day. I think you'll find it useful and interesting, too.

Index

A

accepting friend requests, 51

accounts

account settings, changing, 173-181, 187

deactivating, 182-184

deleting, 184-186

account settings, changing, 173-175

ad settings, 181

applications settings, 178-180

importance of, 187

mobile settings, 180

notifications settings, 177-178

payments settings, 180-181

security settings, 176-177

accounts (Facebook)

creating, 22-23

creating multiple, 29-30

Acquaintances list, 81

acronyms, list of, 101-102

active sessions, 177

Activity Log, viewing/editing, 218-219

adding

friends to custom friends list, 82-83

photo album descriptions, 137

addresses (email), claiming, 107

Adobe Premiere Elements, 147

ad settings, changing, 181

AIM (AOL Instant Messenger), 114

albums. See photo albums

allowing applications, 246

alternate identity, creating, 73-75

America Online, 11

Angry Birds, 245

AOL Instant Messenger (AIM), 114

applications, 10, 243-245

allowing, 246

blocking posts from, 250-251

deleting, 248

editing settings, 248

finding, 245-246

games, 250

hiding updates from, 60-61

list of most useful, 248-250

privacy settings, 195-197

smartphone connections, 278

viewing list of, 247

applications settings, changing, 178-180

app passwords, creating, 177

Apps link, 34

articles, sharing on Facebook, 291-293

asking questions in status updates, 95-96

attaching to status updates

links, 95

photos, 93-94

attachments, sharing, 62-63

P

Y

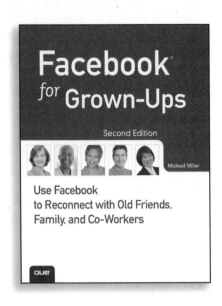

FREE Online Edition

Your purchase of **Facebook for Grown-Ups** includes access to a free online edition for 45 days through the Safari Books Online subscription service. Nearly every Que book is available online through Safari Books Online, along with more than 5,000 other technical books and videos from publishers such as Addison-Wesley Professional, Cisco Press, Exam Cram, IBM Press, O'Reilly, Prentice Hall, and Sams.

SAFARI BOOKS ONLINE allows you to search for a specific answer, cut and paste code, download chapters, and stay current with emerging technologies.

Activate your FREE Online Edition at
www.informit.com/safarifree

> **STEP 1:** Enter the coupon code: MEKBOVH.

> **STEP 2:** New Safari users, complete the brief registration form.
> Safari subscribers, just log in.

If you have difficulty registering on Safari or accessing the online edition, please e-mail customer-service@safaribooksonline.com